HOPE
an Anchor to the Soul

S. MICHAEL WILCOX

DESERET BOOK COMPANY
SALT LAKE CITY, UTAH

Library of Congress Cataloging-in-Publication Data

Wilcox, S. Michael.
   Hope, an anchor to the soul / S. Michael Wilcox.
      p.   cm.
   ISBN 1-57345-542-3
      1. Hope—Religious aspects—Mormon Church.   2. Spiritual life—
Mormon Church.   I. Title.
   BX8643.H67W55   1999
   234'.25—dc21   99-35843
                                                                        CIP

Printed in the United States of America

10 9   8   7   6   5   4   3   2   72082-6483

CONTENTS

CHAPTER ONE

It is good that a man
should both hope
and quietly wait
for the salvation of the Lord.

—LAMENTATIONS 3:26

AN ANCHOR TO THE SOUL

I have heard many sermons on faith and charity and spoken about these topics many times myself, but hope was always a vague subject about which I knew very little. I probably would have described hope as "wishful thinking." I decided to see what I could discover in the scriptures about this pillar of the gospel.

I have learned that hope is an intensely personal thing. It is lodged deep in the human spirit and manifests itself in various ways for different people, but we all need it, and our souls demand it as our bodies crave sleep and nourishment. The images the scriptures use to define hope testify of its absolute necessity in our lives. In these images I began to discover the beauty of hope and the reason it is so important.

THE IMAGES OF HOPE

Four images of hope are particularly compelling. We walk by the light of hope, find protection under the helmet of hope, drink deeply from the river of hope, and brave the wind and storms of

1

life tied securely to the anchor of hope. Thus hope is a guide, a protection, a source of nourishment, and a stabilizing force for our lives. Let us examine these images and the ways the Lord uses them to encourage us in our mortal journey.

In the Book of Mormon hope is shown as a light, and the world is often portrayed as a dark place. Nephi said, "Ye must press forward with a steadfastness in Christ, having a perfect brightness of hope" (2 Nephi 31:20). In the light of hope, our way becomes clear and fear is diminished. "Walk through the darkness of mortality," the Lord seems to say to us, "with my lamp of hope to light your way, to dispel your fears, and to keep you from stumbling or falling."

Hope is also a helmet, and life is a battle against the forces of the world and the adversary. Paul used this image while writing to the Thessalonians. "Let us, who are of the day, be sober, putting on the breastplate of faith and love; and for an helmet, the hope of salvation" (1 Thessalonians 5:8). "When you engage in combat with the forces of the adversary," the Lord seems to instruct us, "wear my helmet of hope to protect you. It will save your lives."

Hope in the Lord is like a constantly flowing river. That beautiful image of hope is found in Jeremiah. "The man that trusteth in man, and maketh flesh his arm, shall be like the heath [a juniper tree] in the desert, and shall not see when good cometh; but shall inhabit the parched places in the wilderness, in a salt land and not inhabited." He contrasted this image of the tree living in the barrenness of the salt desert with "the man that trusteth in the Lord, and whose hope the Lord is. For he shall be as a tree planted by the waters, and that spreadeth out her roots by the river, and shall not see when heat cometh, but her leaf shall be green; and shall not be careful in the year of drought, neither shall cease from yielding fruit" (Jeremiah 17:5-8). We are invited to drink from that river whose waters abound even in times of drought and heat. "Send your roots toward my river of hope and drink deeply," the Lord seems to whisper. "You will survive the severest droughts and the parched places of life."

The fourth image of hope, that of the anchor, we find in the book of Ether. "Wherefore, whoso believeth in God might with surety hope for a better world, . . . which hope cometh of faith, [and] maketh an anchor to the souls of men" (Ether 12:4). Paul called hope "an anchor of the soul, both sure and stedfast" (Hebrews 6:19). Our lives may be likened to an ocean voyage. Perils from storms of wind and waves threaten our vessels. "Cross the ocean of life with my anchor to steady you," the Lord calls. "It will keep you from drifting and drowning."

All four images impart the same vital message. Our happiness and progression depend on our understanding the hope the Lord provides to carry us through mortality, this most critical period of our eternal existence.

In writing about hope I feel somewhat as Nephi may have felt when he declared, "I write the things of my soul" (2 Nephi 4:15). Rather than generalize or try to define abstractions, I have illustrated what the scriptures teach us about hope with examples from people's lives and experiences. I believe that is the best way I can make clear how crucial hope is to all of us. Let us ponder the revealed truths of the scriptures and the experiences of life in search of hope—the light, the helmet, the river, and the anchor.

CHAPTER TWO

Now the God of hope
fill you with all joy
and peace in believing,
that ye may abound in hope,
through the power of the Holy Ghost.

−ROMANS 15:13

THE FOUNDATION
OF FAITH AND HOPE

H ope is always connected to faith, and it is difficult to speak of one without the other. Both faith and hope, to remain constant, must have a solid foundation. The apostle Paul defined faith as "the substance [assurance] of things hoped for, the evidence of things not seen" (Hebrews 11:1; JST Hebrews 11:1). Paul's choice of words is important: Faith is supported by evidence, or assurance; hope must have substance to it. We often think faith and hope are chiefly attached to the emotional aspect of our lives, but they are as concerned with the mind as with the heart.

The definition of faith given by Alma the Younger also links faith to hope and suggests that there must be evidence, or assurance, and substance to it: "If ye have faith ye hope for things which are not seen, which are true" (Alma 32:21). "Truth will cut its own way," Joseph Smith taught (*Teachings of the Prophet Joseph Smith*, sel. Joseph Fielding Smith [Salt Lake City: Deseret

Book, 1976], 313). If we have faith and hope in true principles, they will bring with them their own compelling evidence.

Assurance, or evidence, sufficient to produce a lasting faith is based primarily on reason, authority, and experience, which together provide a firm and solid foundation. They give substance to our hope.

Not only is it important to know something is true but we also need to know why we know it is true. When we say, "I know Jesus is the Christ," we need to be aware of the assurance or evidence that led us to that conclusion. Those who challenge faith have always asked for signs or proof. When Alma the Younger faced Korihor, he faced a man who denied everything in which Alma believed. How did Alma know there was a God? Korihor demanded.

Alma first bore a simple but powerful testimony. "Behold, I say unto you, I know there is a God, and also that Christ shall come" (Alma 30:39). Next, Alma produced his evidence, the substance of his faith and hope. He provided Korihor with four evidences of God's existence. All four are contained in Alma 30:44, and there is substance to them all.

1. "Ye have the testimony of all these thy brethren." Alma first appealed to the experience of the members of the Church. He called as witnesses all the innumerable people who have had personal experiences which demonstrated to them there was a God. These experiences consist of answers to prayer and the hundreds of tiny miracles that happen day by day in ordinary people's lives.

2. "Ye have the testimony of . . . all the holy prophets." In addition to the testimonies of individuals, there have been prophets who walked and talked with God. Alma cited the authority of these men. They saw God and spoke with him. And there is a wonderful consistency in all of their words across time, culture, and continents.

3. "The scriptures are laid before thee." Alma's greatest evi-

dence for God's existence was the scriptures. The words of the scriptures are powerful, the promises are fulfilled, and the principles, when applied, create happiness and peace. In the scriptures we have a combination of all three supports to faith: experience, authority, and reason.

4. "Yea, even the earth, and all things that are upon the face of it, yea, and its motion, yea, and also all the planets which move in their regular form do witness that there is a Supreme Creator." Alma's final evidence was the beauty and order of creation. Such order does not exist independent of a supreme and benevolent being. When Alma examined the wonders of the world around him, his reason told him that God is behind it all.

Other places in the scriptures give similar patterns of evidence supporting testimony. It will strengthen our faith if we will search for the substance and evidence that supports it. Then we will be prepared to do what Peter encouraged when he said, "But sanctify the Lord God in your hearts: and be ready always to give an answer to every man that asketh you a reason of the hope that is in you with meekness and fear" (1 Peter 3:15).

There are reasons for our hope. Let us be aware of them. Then we are planted by the river of hope spoken of by Jeremiah. During the dry seasons of our lives, when fears and doubts assail our faith, our hope will not die nor wither. Its deep roots will draw nourishment from experience, authority, and reason. As we study the scriptures, we will find we have many reasons, much evidence, and great substance to sustain our hope.

CHAPTER THREE

*Wherefore, we search the prophets,
and we have many revelations
and the spirit of prophecy;
and having all these witnesses
we obtain a hope,
and our faith becometh unshaken.*

—JACOB 4:6

THE SUBSTANCE OF HOPE

Faith is the first principle of the gospel, yet, as Mormon taught, without hope we cannot develop faith. He said to his people: "I would speak unto you concerning hope. How is it that ye can attain unto faith, save ye shall have hope?" He then explained what we should hope for. "I say unto you that ye shall have hope through the atonement of Christ . . . to be raised unto life eternal" (Moroni 7:40–41).

THE NATURE OF THE FATHER AND THE SON

Joseph Smith taught that three things were necessary to have faith in God sufficient for life and salvation: "First, the idea that he [God] actually exists. . . . Secondly, a *correct* idea of his character, perfections, and attributes. . . . Thirdly, an actual knowledge that the course of life which he is pursuing is according to his will" (*Lectures on Faith*, comp. N. B. Lundwall [Salt Lake City: N. B. Lundwall, n.d.], 33). Hope is centered in the second of these, "a *correct* idea of [God's] character, perfections, and attributes."

Without a correct knowledge of the God we worship, we will not be able to develop either hope or faith. We worship the Savior not only because he is God, but because he is the kind of God he is. A principal role of the scriptures, therefore, is to give us a clear picture of the nature of the Father and his Son. Our hope rests in that nature. They have all the noblest attributes of character, and they have them in perfection.

When I was in junior high, I forgot to take with me to school an important assignment for one of my classes. There was no one home for me to call and no way for me to go home to get it. I remember the completely hopeless feeling I had going to class. My friend said, "Maybe he will let you bring it in tomorrow." I knew better. I knew the character and reputation of that particular teacher. No excuse was ever acceptable. I failed the assignment.

Years later, another teacher, a similar situation, yet this time, I knew the teacher would grant me a day of grace. I knew her character and reputation, yet that knowledge did not induce me to take advantage of her mercy. I respected her too much to impose upon her mercy deliberately.

Our knowledge of the character and reputation of Christ allows us to "come boldly unto the throne of grace, that we may obtain mercy" (Hebrews 4:16), yet our love and respect for him keeps us from deliberately imposing on his goodness by disobeying with the intent to repent later. The prophets describe that goodness in great detail so that our hope may be established on a firm foundation.

"THE GOODNESS OF GOD"

King Benjamin spoke of the qualities of the Savior: "Ye have come to a knowledge of the goodness of God, and his matchless power, and his wisdom, and his patience, and his long-suffering towards the children of men: and also, the atonement which has been prepared from the foundation of the world" (Mosiah 4:6). He reminded his people they had "come to the knowledge of the glory of God, . . . have known of his goodness and have tasted of his love, and have received a remission of your sins" (Mosiah 4:11).

Nephi spoke frequently about the character of Jesus, emphasizing, as did Benjamin, his patience and long-suffering, especially as these perfections related to the Atonement: "They scourge him, and he suffereth it; and they smite him, and he suffereth it. Yea, they spit upon him, and he suffereth it, because of his loving kindness and his long-suffering towards the children of men" (1 Nephi 19:9).

Nephi spoke also of the Savior's willingness to extend his kindness to all mankind. "He doeth not anything save it be for the benefit of the world; for he loveth the world, even that he layeth down his own life. . . . Wherefore, he commandeth none that they shall not partake of his salvation. Behold, doth he cry unto any, saying: Depart from me? Behold, I say unto you Nay; but he saith: Come unto me all ye ends of the earth. . . . Hath he commanded any that they should not partake of his salvation? Behold, I say unto you, Nay; but he hath given it free for all men. . . . Behold, hath the Lord commanded any that they should not partake of his goodness? Behold I say unto you, Nay; but all men are privileged the one like unto the other, and none are forbidden" (2 Nephi 26:24-25; 27-28). Nephi's repeated use of the question-and-answer form is designed to emphasize the Savior's love. We need not fear that he will turn us away.

Alma the Younger was certainly acquainted with the mercy and compassion of Christ. While teaching the rebellious citizens of Ammonihah, who might have reminded Alma of his own younger self, he explained the mercy of Christ: "And not many days hence the Son of God shall come in his glory; and his glory shall be the glory of the Only Begotten of the Father, full of grace, equity, and truth, full of patience, mercy, and long-suffering, quick to hear the cries of his people and to answer their prayers" (Alma 9:26).

David beautifully portrayed in the Psalms the mercy of Christ. One of the most powerful, Psalm 103, contains the following description of Jesus. "The Lord is merciful and gracious, slow to anger, and plenteous in mercy. He will not always chide. . . . He hath not dealt with us after our sins; nor rewarded us according to our iniquities. For as the heaven is high above the earth, so great is his mercy toward them that fear him. As far as the east is from the west, so far hath he removed our transgressions from us. Like as a father pitieth his children, so the Lord pitieth them that fear him. For he knoweth our frame; he remembereth that we are dust" (Psalm 103:8–14).

John the Beloved inspired hope in the early Saints when he testified: "We have known and believed the love that God hath to us. God is love; and he that dwelleth in love dwelleth in God, and God in him" (1 John 4:16). Mormon, lamenting over the fall of his people, also spoke of the love of Christ: "O ye fair ones, how could ye have rejected that Jesus, who stood with open arms to receive you!" (Mormon 6:17). And Isaiah summed up all the qualities of the Savior with one word: "And his name shall be called Wonderful" (Isaiah 9:6).

We could compile many, many verses like these, all showing the nature and perfections of the Savior. We worship him because he possesses these qualities in their perfection, and in them we find the source of our hope. Brigham Young once commented that "only a few men on the earth understand the charity that fills the bosom of our Savior" (*Journal of Discourses*, 26 vols. [London: Latter-day Saints' Book Depot, 1856–81], 8:175). Like Jeremiah's river, the charity of Christ never ceases to send its life-sustaining moisture to our roots.

"O WRETCHED MAN THAT I AM"

Like us, Nephi was sometimes very aware of his short-comings. He desired to glory in the wonders of the gospel and delight and ponder on the great truths of the scriptures. "Nevertheless, notwithstanding the great goodness of the Lord . . . my heart exclaimeth: O wretched man that I am! Yea, my heart sorroweth because of my flesh; my soul grieveth because of mine iniquities. I am encompassed about, because of the temptations and the sins which do so easily beset me. And when I desire to rejoice, my heart groaneth because of my sins; nevertheless, I know in whom I have trusted" (2 Nephi 4:17–19).

Many times we feel exactly as Nephi felt. We try and try always to do right, but "temptations and sins . . . so easily beset" us, and our hearts groan. These feelings are common to all mankind. The great artist Michelangelo wrote, "Despite Thy promises, O Lord, 'twould seem too much to hope that even love like Thine can overlook my countless wanderings." Benjamin Franklin expressed his own efforts at righteousness with the following words: "I conceived the bold and arduous project of arriving at moral perfection. I wished to live without committing any fault at any time. . . . But I soon found I had undertaken a task of more difficulty than I had imagined. While my care was employed in guarding against one fault, I was often suprised by another. . . . I was surprised to find myself so much fuller of faults than I had imagined" (*Autobiography of Benjamin Franklin,* [London, Heron Books], 73, 79).

As we have seen, when Nephi faced the reality of his own humanity and weakness, he found the hope to continue his quest for exaltation in the God in whom he trusted. He had faith in the goodness, mercy, and compassion of his Savior. Likewise, our own faith in the Savior resides in these qualities. Our hope germinates in the rich soil of his perfections.

CLIMB WITHOUT FEAR

I have a son who enjoys rock climbing. It is a dangerous sport, one in which a mistake may result in serious consequences. I have learned from him there are two basic rules to follow. The first is always to check your equipment before you climb. The second rule is based on the first. If your equipment is sound, trust it and climb without fear. Fear saps strength, and when rock climbing, you must have all the strength your body possesses to reach the top.

Nephi tells us we must "press forward with a steadfastness in Christ, having a perfect brightness of hope" (2 Nephi 31:20). As we climb to perfection, we must trust the rope that supports us. It is a rope of love, mercy, patience, goodness, and wisdom. We must trust it and climb with hope, not fear, or our strength will slowly be drained from us. Jesus himself told Enoch, "Whoso . . . climbeth up by me shall never fall" (Moses 7:53).

Isaiah used a beautiful metaphor for Christ that relates to our ability to trust him. "I will fasten him as a nail in a sure place; and he shall be for a glorious throne to his father's house. And they shall hang upon him all the glory of his father's house, the offspring and the issue, all vessels of small quantity, from the vessels of cups, even to all the vessels of flagons" (Isaiah 22:23–24).

If we drive a nail into a soft piece of sandstone and then put great weight on it, the nail will not hold, for the nail will not have been driven into a sure place. But if we drive it into a solid piece of granite, the nail will hold. It is in a sure place. Christ is like that nail. His mercy and willingness to forgive are secure. His atonement is eternal. We can trust that truth.

The scriptures often liken vessels to people. In Isaiah's metaphor, the nail is able to support any vessel from the smallest cup to the greatest flagon. We might picture the various vessels in a household suspended from a nail driven into a wall. This image suggests that anyone from the tiniest child to the mightiest king can hope for salvation through the atoning love of Christ.

"SEVEN TIMES IN A DAY"

When a person rose in authority in the ancient world, his father's whole household rose with him. Thus uncles, cousins, brothers and sisters, and children found positions of authority and favor in the new dynasty. Isaiah's words might also imply this situation. Conversely, if the person fell from power, all his dependents fell with him. We can be assured our King will establish an everlasting kingdom and we can rely on his strength.

The Savior delights in forgiveness and wants all of his Father's household to share positions of authority in his eternal kingdom. The parable of the prodigal son testifies of this truth. There is no more powerful description of God than that of the father running to his repentant child when he is "yet a great way off" (Luke 15:20) and embracing him as a son. Every time I read that verse, I feel both the deep repentance of the son and the loving forgiveness of the father. Wretched and unworthy as the son felt, he could trust in his father's love. When "he began to be in want . . . and no man gave unto him" (Luke 15:14, 16), he knew deep in his soul there was someone who would always accept him, for whom forgiveness was a great joy (D&C 18:13). He need only return.

Sometimes we hesitate to return because the sins that so easily beset us are repeated sins. When we do something wrong or when we fail to do right, we go to the Lord seeking his forgiveness. It is usually not too difficult or painful to go to him the first time. If we are sincere in our repentance, the Lord will grant our request and extend forgiveness. We are then counseled to "go, and sin no more" (John 8:11). We stay righteous for a time, but then our weaknesses are manifested again, and we repeat our error. Now it is more difficult to petition the throne of God, but we are driven to our knees by our need to find relief. Once again we are forgiven.

Sometimes we struggle with our sins for many years. In desperation we may covenant with God that we will not repeat them. Our desire is sincere, our covenant well intentioned, but despite these efforts to control our weakness, we slip again. Now it is very painful to return to ask for forgiveness. What must the Lord think of us?

How many times may we go to the Lord for relief, forgiveness, and understanding? We receive hope in the answer the Savior himself taught: "If [thy brother] trespass against thee seven times in a day, and seven times in a day turn again to thee, saying, I repent; thou shalt forgive him" (Luke 17:4). The Lord would not require of us a standard he himself is unwilling to live. We may go to him seven times in a day and each time he will forgive us, saying, "Neither do I condemn thee: go, and sin no more" (John 8:11). If the Savior forgives us, then we must not make ourselves a higher judge by refusing to forgive ourselves.

Nevertheless, we must not let this divine level of mercy become an excuse for sin. Paul taught us the correct response we should have as we trust in the great goodness of Christ: "Despisest thou the riches of His goodness and forbearance and long-suffering; not knowing that the goodness of God leadeth thee to repentance?" (Romans 2:4). In other words, the goodness of Christ was meant to turn us to him without fear, seeking his mercy, not to become a license to sin. The phrase "I can always repent," though true if the repentance is sincere, is a mockery of the Savior's love and sacrifice when used as a justification for disobedience. We must not take advantage of his patience, but trust it when our desires for improvement and cleansing rise from the deepest feelings of our hearts.

I DON'T REMEMBER THAT

We all need assurances that we are forgiven and that the Lord is pleased with our efforts. Our hope must be kept alive. We must be reminded of the goodness of the God we worship. Are we not told to always remember him each week when we take the sacrament? Much of that weekly remembrance is an expression of gratitude, but it is also an invitation for hope.

From time to time in our lives, the Lord graciously allows us to know of his goodness and taste of his love (Mosiah 4:11). The scriptures contain many wonderful verses that will keep our hope burning brightly if we reflect on them and allow the Spirit to testify of their truths. The Lord promised that if we will "turn from all [our] sins" and "do that which is lawful and right," then "all [our] transgressions that [we have] committed, they shall not be mentioned unto [us]: in [our] righteousness that [we have] done [we] shall live" (Ezekiel 18:21–22). It is a human tendency to focus on failures and weaknessess instead of on the victories and good deeds of our lives. It is imperative that we learn to see ourselves not at our worst moments but in the accumulation of our most typical and best moments.

With that perspective in mind, we might visualize a conversation with our Eternal Judge. I do not suggest that the following is an accurate image of the Judgment, but I believe that the Lord has recorded faithfully every tiny thing we do and say that is righteous and that his mercy consists in focusing on the good actions of our lives. In that context, then, imagine you are seated in a comfortable chair next to the Judge, who will interview you about your efforts in life. At first you are somewhat apprehensive. Perhaps the first question you are asked is, "Did you proclaim the gospel?" With some anxiety you respond, "I tried." He answers, "Let us see." A scene is then opened up before you which keeps changing as you witness memories from your life. You are shown everything you have ever done to share the gospel. You see efforts with your friends, full-time missions, stake and ward missionary efforts. You are shown certain individuals you knew and with whom you shared the gospel or engaged in gospel conversations. You see many acts of kindness and fellowship with people from your neighborhoods or places of employment. Portrayed before you are the times you have spoken of the Church with others who were seated next to you on airline flights. Tender scenes when you have supported your own children on missions are also faithfully preserved. Every tiny detail of your life is recorded that has anything to do with proclaiming the gospel.

When he is finished, the Judge turns to you and asks once again: "Did you proclaim the gospel?"

You look at him, still in rather a tentative manner, not quite sure of yourself, and answer, "Yes?" You probably follow that hesitant yes by asking, "But what about all my failures?"

"Tell me your failures," he replies.

You recount to him all the times you felt you had failed to proclaim the gospel correctly or often enough. It seems you can remember them all so well. He listens patiently and then, smiling, assures you, "I don't remember that." You look up at him in surprise. How could he remember all your efforts and yet forget your failures?

Without giving you more time to think, he may then ask, "Did you redeem the dead?"

"I tried," you answer him.

"Let us see."

Once again the scenes of your life open up. You see recorded every effort you have ever made regarding the redemption of the dead. You see trips to the temple with your family. You see yourself in the Family History Library searching records. You see yourself testifying about the blessings of the temple and of laboring for your ancestors within its walls. Every tiny detail you have ever accomplished regarding the temple has been carefully recorded, including the gathering of family histories and journals.

When these scenes are ended, the Judge turns to you once again. "Did you redeem the dead?"

You answer again tentatively, "Yes, but what about all my failures?"

"Tell me your failures," he replies.

You tell him about the times you missed attending the temple, or duplicated ordinance work, or sealed the wrong people, or followed the wrong lines. You should have spent more time in research or in striving to discover the meaning behind the temple's powerful symbols. You tell him of the times you dozed during the session instead of being alert and attentive. It is such a relief to tell him everything. He listens patiently and then replies, "I don't remember that."

You look at him once more in surprise, but before you can say anything he asks you a third question. "Did you perfect the Saints?"

"I tried," you answer.

"Let us see."

Once more the scenes of memory open to your view. Every effort you have ever made in working with the members of the Church is recorded. You see yourself home or visiting teaching and fulfilling Church callings. You have taught Sunday School, Primary, Relief Society, the deacons, or the Webelos. You have accompanied young men and women to camp or youth conference. You see helpful conversations and tiny acts of service.

When the scenes are completed the Judge turns to you and asks, "Did you perfect the Saints?"

Hesitantly, and yet with growing confidence, you answer, "Yes, but what about my failures? What about the times I missed home teaching, or offended another member of the Church, or failed to do my duty well enough?"

He listens patiently, only to reply, "I don't remember that."

The interview continues in this manner through many other questions, perhaps including such questions as, "Were you a good husband or wife? Were you a good mother or father? Were you a good son or daughter to your parents and a good brother or sister to the other children in your family? Did you follow the counsel of the prophets?" Each time you answer, "I tried," he shows you the positive things you have done in each area. When you tell him your failures, he continues to respond, "I don't remember that." Every time he repeats those simple words, hope burns more brightly in your heart, and you more deeply understand the many descriptions of his character recorded in the scriptures.

Because he is good and kind and merciful, we all may hope to have a place in the kingdom of our Father in Heaven. Consider the profound meaning of the scriptures that say, "I, the Lord, remember them no more," (D&C 58:42) and "They shall not be mentioned unto him: in his righteousness that he hath done he shall live" (Ezekiel 18:22). Over the years it has become obvious to me that the Savior is more interested in the positive parts of our lives than in the negative parts. When we understand that about our own relationship with the Lord, we will feel him encouraging us to treat others in the same manner. Let us remember, very carefully, every detail of each others' good qualities and efforts and be quick to forget perceived failures or infractions of the law. We may then anticipate that the Lord will grant us the widest latitude of mercy.

THE REAL YOU

Often we hear the expression, "Now I know the real you." What is the real you? Far too often the real you is taken to mean what you are at your worst. We need to challenge that idea. The real you is you at your very best, not at your worst. In the parable of the prodigal son, the Savior told us that when the younger son "came to himself" (Luke 15:17), his real self, he returned home. The "real" younger son knew where he belonged and finally returned to his father. The clearest and most true evaluation of ourselves must encompass our best moments and qualities, not our worst. Focusing on our failures and weaknesses may cause us to despair, whereas focusing on our successes and strengths will kindle the perfect brightness of hope Nephi described. We can be assured that our Father in Heaven and the Savior prefer to focus on the most positive aspects of our characters.

We were created in the image of God. That refers not only to the physical but also to the qualities of our mind and heart. We may not yet have the characteristics of God in perfection, but the first stirrings of those feelings and attributes are part of our birthright. They represent our real souls, for which we must struggle against the tendencies of the natural man.

CHAPTER FOUR

I will bear him up
as on eagles' wings;
and he shall beget glory and honor
to himself and unto my name.

–DOCTRINE AND COVENANTS 124:18

HOPE FOR THE JOURNEY

I was never very good at athletics when I was young. I spent most of my young years envious of boys who could play sports with ease and confidence. Of all athletic endeavors, however, I dreaded track and field the most.

I remember the coach lining us up at the starting line, firing the starting pistol, and clicking the stopwatch as we ran down the track towards the first turn. The stopwatch was my enemy. Until the first turn I could usually stay in the pack, but somewhere along the back stretch my wind would begin to die and my legs to ache. Boy after boy would pass me. The harder I tried to catch up, the more exhausted I became. As the first runners crossed the finish line, the coach called out their times. More boys passed me, my lungs burned, and only the thought of being laughed at prevented me from quitting altogether. Finally the ordeal was over, but my time was never good enough, and my grades in gym reflected my failures.

"RUN WITH PATIENCE"

On several occasions, the apostle Paul compared life to a race. To the Corinthian Saints he said, "Know ye not that they which run in a race run all, but one receiveth the prize? So run, that ye may obtain" (1 Corinthians 9:24). In his last epistle to Timothy, Paul referred to his own life as a race. "I have fought a good fight, I have finished my course, I have kept the faith" (2 Timothy 4:7).

We often view our pursuit of perfection as a race. We want to run to perfection, racing against an eternal stopwatch that continues ticking. At times we feel exhausted because we are not progressing fast enough. We look ahead at the other runners, comparing their qualities and characteristics to our own, and a spiritual fatigue settles over us akin to the physical one I experienced watching the other boys move to the finish line far ahead of me.

In Hebrews, Paul again compares life to a race, but he counsels us to run that race in a way we might not ordinarily associate with rapid, fast-paced striving. "Let us lay aside every weight, and the sin which doth so easily beset us, and let us run with patience the race that is set before us, looking unto Jesus the author and finisher of our faith . . . lest ye be wearied and faint in your minds" (Hebrews 12:1–3).

The race of life must be run with patience with our focus set on the Savior, who waits at the finish line, or else we may become weary and faint. The race of life is not a sprint but an effort that demands endurance. Notice that Paul speaks of a weariness of mind, a loss of hope that may lead us to faint before our race is won.

HE "SHALL GENTLY LEAD" THEM

We now turn to Isaiah for understanding about our striving for perfection and what the Lord promises he will do for us if we focus on endurance instead of speed.

In the early chapters of Isaiah, the Lord chastens his people for their worldliness, but a definite shift in tone comes in the fortieth chapter in the very first lines: "Comfort ye, comfort ye my people, saith your God. Speak ye comfortably to Jerusalem, and cry unto her, . . . that her iniquity is pardoned" (Isaiah 40:1-2). Throughout the next chapters, the Savior speaks some of the most comforting words in holy writ. With our race of life in mind, let us seek to understand what the Savior will do so that we may "press forward . . . having a perfect brightness of hope" (2 Nephi 31:20).

I have often turned to Isaiah's comforting words when I begin to question my own ability to endure to the finish line:

"Behold, the Lord God will come with strong hand, and his arm shall rule for him: behold his reward is with him, and his work before him. He shall feed his flock like a shepherd: he shall gather the lambs with his arm, and carry them in his bosom, and shall gently lead those that are with young" (Isaiah 40:10-11).

The Old Testament image of the Savior as a shepherd is beautiful in its fulness, but Isaiah's use of the word *gently* has struck the deepest chords in my heart. It removes the sense of hurry with its accompanying anxiety that we are not progressing rapidly enough. "Gently we will walk the path of life," the Savior seems to whisper to us. There is sufficient time to reach our goal. Fear saps us of needed strength, and Christ's arm is strong enough for those times when our own strength begins to fail us.

The Lord makes similar assurances in other places in the scriptures. One of my favorites is in Doctrine and Covenants 78: "Verily, verily, I say unto you, ye are little children, and ye have not as yet understood how great blessings the Father hath in his own hands and prepared for you; And ye cannot bear all things now; nevertheless, be of good cheer, for I will lead you along. The kingdom is yours and the blessings thereof are yours, and the riches of eternity are yours. And he who receiveth all things with thankfulness shall be made glorious. . . . Wherefore, do the things which I have commanded you, saith your Redeemer . . . who prepareth all things before he taketh you" (vv. 17-20).

We are "little children," the lambs of which Isaiah spoke. We are encouraged to be thankful and of good cheer. Our Shepherd has prepared all things and promises he will lead us along. Although we have not yet reached our goal, the kingdom, the blessings, and the riches of eternity will eventually be ours.

"MOUNT UP WITH WINGS AS EAGLES"

In the same chapter of Isaiah in which we are assured the Savior will gently lead us along, we are also promised he will infuse us with strength beyond our natural ability. This promise is given with energy and conviction that we might believe it and run with hope:

"Has thou not known? hast thou not heard, that the everlasting God, the Lord, the Creator of the ends of the earth, fainteth not, neither is weary? there is no searching of his understanding. He giveth power to the faint; and to them that have no might he increaseth strength. Even the youths shall faint and be weary, and the young men shall utterly fall: but they that wait upon the Lord shall renew their strength; they shall mount up with wings as eagles; they shall run, and not be weary; and they shall walk, and not faint" (Isaiah 40:28-31).

From time to time in life, we will have experiences that will strengthen us and help us persevere. They do not usually come according to our own timetable, but in the Lord's divine wisdom they come when we most need them. If we "wait upon the Lord," our strength will be renewed. We should not be surprised that we experience spiritual fatigue; after all the prize for which we run is godhood. We cannot obtain it without the Lord's help. Having traveled the path himself, the Savior understands, "and to them that have no might he increaseth strength" (Isaiah 40:29).

"FEAR THOU NOT; FOR I AM WITH THEE"

All of us experience various fears. Some are afraid of heights or of small, closed-in places. Some fear various animals, reptiles, or insects. Public speaking is very difficult for many. Others dread being alone. Like everyone else, I have my own collection of fears, but there is one I share with many Latter-day Saints. It is a fear perhaps best expressed by Joseph Smith himself when he said, "I often felt condemned for my weakness and imperfections" (Joseph Smith–History 1:29). The greatest fear for many of us is the fear of spiritual failure—not of massive failure, but of not quite measuring up to the standard desired by our Father in Heaven. We're afraid we'll miss heaven by inches, not yards.

I can recall many times when I tried my best to get an *A* in one of my classes at school and then missed it by a few percentage points. Many times the teacher would write on my test or paper the words, "Good effort." This comment was kindly intended and meant to soften the blow of missing the highest grade, but it was rarely comforting. Often, I would say to myself, "I don't know how I could have studied harder or put more time into my work. I guess I'm just a *B+* student."

We often see ourselves as *B+* types. We are not bad people, but we experience sufficient unease about our character to feel the constant pressure of the weight of our "shortcomings"—as we like to call our sins. We try hard, but our efforts often fall short. Joseph Smith said he was not "guilty of any great or malignant sins. A disposition to commit such was never in my nature," but he did things he felt were "not consistent with that character which ought to be maintained by one who was called of God"

(Joseph Smith–History 1:28). I am confident all of us can relate to the Prophet Joseph's words.

In our more anxious moments, it is not hard for us to imagine the Lord saying, "You made a great effort, and your work is good. I cannot give you an *A*, but you are a solid *B+*, and I have a lovely kingdom for *B+* people." In our worst moments of fear, the *B+* slips into the *B-* and *C+* range, and our hope falters.

During these times, we may receive great comfort from the words of the Lord as written by Isaiah: "Fear thou not; for I am with thee: be not dismayed; for I am thy God: I will strengthen thee; yea, I will help thee; yea, I will uphold thee with the right hand of my righteousness. . . . For I the Lord thy God will hold thy right hand, saying unto thee, Fear not; I will help thee" (Isaiah 41:10, 13).

As we run our race of life, not only will he lead us along gently but he will also hold our hand and calm our fears. How comforting these promises are when we apply them to our *B+* personalities and our unique fears.

How often do we plead with the Lord in our prayers on behalf of ourselves and our families, saying, "Please Lord, don't let us fail. Whatever is needed in thy divine wisdom to mold us in the pattern thou desirest, we accept; but please don't let us fail." He will answer this prayer with those comforting words of Isaiah: "Fear thou not; for I am with thee: be not dismayed."

"HE SHALL NOT . . . BE DISCOURAGED"

When my son was little, I tried very hard to teach him how to swim. He had a great fear of the water, and it was an agony just getting him into the pool. For years we struggled to help him overcome that fear, but all our efforts met with failure. When he stood at the edge of the pool looking into the water, his heart froze with fear. Sometimes during those years of effort, my son sensed my frustration—and I have to admit there were days when I wanted to throw up my hands and walk away, accepting the fact that he would never learn how to swim. Though he never voiced it, I often saw in my son's eyes the plea, "Don't give up on me, Dad! I want to swim." I could never refuse that look, and once again we would face the water and his fear.

Because we sometimes get discouraged with each other or with our own progress, if we are not careful we might attribute that earthly discouragement to the Lord. In times of our greatest discouragement we are afraid the Lord might give up on us. We plead with him to be patient while we try again. The comforting words of Isaiah fill us with hope. Speaking of the Savior, Isaiah wrote, "He shall not fail nor be discouraged, till he have set judgment in the earth: and the isles shall wait for his law" (Isaiah 42:4). If he does not get discouraged about the whole earth, he will not get discouraged with us as long as we desire to keep trying. Discouragement is not one of the Lord's attributes. If we know that, our hope can remain constant.

I WILL NOT FORSAKE THEM

We have seen blind individuals walking without a guide or any other help except a white cane. I have often admired their ability to learn their environment and move from place to place with calm and security. How would we feel if we were blind and were taken along an unfamiliar path? If a friend volunteered to help us walk that path, we would need to know two things: Does this person know the way, and will he or she remain with us throughout the journey? What a fearful thing it would be to be unable to see, placed on a road we had never traveled, and then forsaken.

The Savior's promises in Isaiah offer assurance that our hope in Christ will not be in vain. "I will bring the blind by a way that they knew not; I will lead them in paths that they have not known: I will make darkness light before them, and crooked things straight. These things will I do unto them, and not forsake them" (Isaiah 42:16).

We have never walked the paths of mortality before. We are spirit beings who live in an unfamiliar world, but we have faith in One who has walked its paths and knows the way. With confidence and trust, despite our "blindness," we may proceed, knowing our guide will never forsake us. "Be of good cheer, little children; for I am in your midst, and I have not forsaken you" (D&C 61:36).

The Savior promises that he will continue to work with us until we are perfect, as he himself is perfect. The road may be hard, but he has paid the price for us to receive exaltation. As long as we are willing to continue, he will labor with us.

Ultimately, he cannot accept anything short of perfection. All of us must obey the command he gave to his Nephite disciples when he said, "Therefore, what manner of men ought ye to be? Verily I say unto you, even as I am" (3 Nephi 27:27). He is patient and long-suffering. He will not become discouraged nor leave us. We have his assurance that he will continue to labor with us until we have accomplished everything that is necessary.

I am reminded of what the chairman of my doctoral committee told me as I began to work on my dissertation, "Rest assured, you will receive your degree if you want it. I will not allow you to face the final examinations until I know you will pass, and I will not quit working with you until you reach that point." You can imagine how grateful I was to that man for his commitment to me. It allowed me to progress with confidence and hope.

"I WILL CARRY . . . YOU"

I was once given a gift of a story recorded in beautiful handwriting and beautifully framed. I had often heard this story repeated in talks and firesides. It tells of two sets of footprints in the sand, one belonging to the narrator of the story and the other to the Savior. They represent the journey of life. At one point one of the sets of footprints disappears. This happened at a particularly difficult time in the narrator's life, and he asked the Savior why He left him during this time of trial. The Savior replied, "That is when I carried you."

As comforting as this story is, the Lord goes even further in the writings of Isaiah. "Hearken unto me, O house of Jacob, and all the remnant of the house of Israel, which are borne by me from the belly, which are carried from the womb and even to your old age I am he; and even to hoar hairs will I carry you: I have made, and I will bear; even I will carry, and will deliver you" (Isaiah 46:3-4).

It is natural to carry an infant but not a mature adult. In truth, the more we mature the more self-sufficient we desire to be. Yet the Lord promises he will bear us "even to . . . old age," because he "made" us. In one sense, there are never two sets of footprints in the sand, only one.

We face the weaknesses of our own character, often feeling we should have overcome them years ago. Why do they still trouble us? We have trials and hardships that drain our strength. Our pride often gets in the way of fully turning to the Savior for help. Nevertheless, there are times in all of our lives when we must turn to the Lord and simply say, "Lord, I have done all I can." At these times we must have the humility to allow the Lord to carry us even as a father carries his child.

"WHEN THOU WALKEST THROUGH THE FIRE"

As we run the race of life, we encounter trials and obstacles we must overcome. Often in the times of our deepest trials we feel completely alone. We look for comfort, and the Lord answers us:

"When thou passest through the waters, I will be with thee; and through the rivers, they shall not overflow thee: when thou walkest through the fire, thou shalt not be burned; neither shall the flame kindle upon thee. For I am the Lord thy God, the Holy One of Israel, thy Saviour" (Isaiah 43:2-3).

Many years ago I read an article by the actor Jimmy Stewart containing cherished memories of his father. I was deeply impressed with the faith in God his father instilled in him during World War II. It is the finest illustration of Isaiah's words I know.

"During World War II, I enlisted in the Air Corps and became part of a bomber squadron. When we were ready to fly overseas, Dad came to the farewell ceremonies in Sioux City, Iowa. We were very self-conscious with each other . . . trying to conceal our awareness that, starting tomorrow, he could no longer walk with me. At the time of the greatest crisis in my life, he would have to stand aside. . . . I knew he was searching for a final word to sustain me, but he couldn't find it. . . . We embraced, then he turned and walked quickly away. Only after he had gone did I realize that he had put a small envelope in my pocket.

"That night alone in my bunk, I opened and read, 'My dear Jim, soon after you read this letter, you will be on your way to the worst sort of danger. I have had this in mind for a long time and I am very concerned. . . . But, Jim, I am banking on the enclosed copy of the 91st Psalm. The thing that takes the place of fear and worry is the promise in these words. I am staking my faith in these words. I feel sure that God will lead you through this mad experience. . . . God bless you and keep. . . .'

"I wept. In the envelope there was also a small booklet bearing the title THE SECRET PLACE—A Key to the 91st Psalm. I began to read it. From that day, the little booklet was always with me. Before every bombing raid over Europe, I read some of it, and with each reading the meaning deepened for me.

"'I will say of the Lord, He is my refuge and my fortress. . . .

His truth shall be thy shield and buckler. Thou shalt not be afraid for the terror by night, nor for the arrow that flieth by day. . . . For He shall give His angels charge over thee, to keep thee in all thy ways. They shall bear thee up in their hands, lest thou dash thy foot against a stone.'

"And I was borne up. Dad had committed me to God, but I felt the presence of both throughout the war" ("This Was My Father," *McCalls,* May 1964).

"SINCE THOU WAST PRECIOUS IN MY SIGHT"

Why does the Lord do all these wonderful things for us? The Lord himself answers that question: "Since thou wast precious in my sight, thou hast been honourable, and I have loved thee" (Isaiah 43:4). I once heard Dr. Arthur Henry King say that one of the most profound discoveries of his life was the realization that the woman he loved, loved him. Those words had a profound impact on my life, because I too had experienced this same discovery and thought it the most wonderful and powerful of truths.

Yet, there is a more profound and deeper discovery, one we must receive in our hearts and accept with all our souls. It is the truth that the Savior and God whom we love actually loves us. He who is so precious to us feels that we are precious to him. My mind had long ago accepted that truth, but it was not until I read the words of Isaiah one afternoon when my hope was not shining with perfect brightness that its power sank deep in my heart. With all our shortcomings, we still are precious to him, and he loves us.

"TO WHOM WILL YE LIKEN ME?"

More than once in Isaiah the Lord asks, "To whom will ye liken me, and make me equal, and compare me, that we may be like?" (Isaiah 46:5; 40:18). The Lord answers this question more than a dozen times. "There is no God else beside me; a just God and a Saviour; there is none beside me. Look unto me, and be ye saved, all the ends of the earth: for I am God, and there is none else. . . . Unto me every knee shall bow, and every tongue shall swear" (Isaiah 45:21–23). Our knees shall bow in reverence, and our tongues shall profess our love and gratitude.

As we put all the promises of Isaiah together, what hope is engendered for our journey! The Lord will lead us gently along the path to perfection. He will strengthen us when we feel weary. He will silence our fears, for he will hold our hands. He knows no discouragement. He will not give up on us nor forsake us: he will be by our side through all our trials, and if need be, he will carry us from birth to our old age. Truly there is no God like him; there is no comfort or hope equal to that which he inspires. Let us ever remember the words of the Lord to Isaiah: "Comfort ye, Comfort ye my people, saith your God" (Isaiah 40:1).

CHAPTER FIVE

Why art thou cast down,
O my soul?
and why art thou disquieted within me?
hope in God:
for I shall yet praise him,
who is the health of my countenance,
and my God.

—PSALM 43:5

HOPE IN OUR PROGRESSION

I have always pictured the strait and narrow path as climbing. In my mind it is a mountain path, not one that crosses a prairie. The Lord told Enoch, "Whoso cometh in at the gate and climbeth up by me shall never fall" (Moses 7:53). I enjoy climbing mountains and have felt that exhilaration that comes when you stand at the very peak of a high mountain after a strenuous effort to reach the top. I have learned during those climbs how to read my own thoughts and emotions.

During the early stages of the climb, I rarely want to complete it. I usually cannot see the peak, and the thought of the tremendous effort the climb will demand is mentally fatiguing. If I am backpacking, that is when the load on my back feels the heaviest. How can I possibly carry this uphill for so many miles? I can give myself a hundred reasons why the whole idea of the climb is foolish and why I would be much happier to turn around and comfortably enjoy the view from the foot of the mountain.

I must talk myself out of these thoughts because they make climbing more difficult. I have learned how necessary it is for me to stop for a moment occasionally, catch my breath, and look down the mountain to see how far I've come. That creates a grand feeling of accomplishment that gives me a second wind. It gives me a taste of the overwhelming feeling I know I will receive at the very top, where the view below is so inspiring.

I have also learned to wait for a certain moment on the trail. I know it will come, but I do not always know at which point in the climb. It is the moment when I see the peak up close for the first time. A strong desire to stand on top of it is born at this time, and from that moment on nothing will stop me. At that point I stop looking down and focus all my attention on the peak. I will not look down again until I have arrived at the top.

The path to exaltation is much like climbing a mountain. Perfection of character and soul look distant when we begin our journey. It seems much easier simply to live a decent life at the foot of the mountain. Usually the first year after conversion is most challenging to converts, and the teen years and early twenties are most challenging to those who are born in the Church. These are the times when the climb looks most laborious. Brigham Young said: "When the Gospel is preached to the honest in heart they receive it by faith, but when they obey it labor is required. To practice the Gospel requires time, faith, the heart's affections and a great deal of labor. Here many stop" (*Journal of Discourses*, 26 vols. [London: Latter-day Saints' Book Depot, 1856–81], 16:40).

One of the great secrets in continuing our climb toward perfection is to turn around occasionally on the trail and see how far we have come. These moments give us a spiritual second wind. Our progression will take time, but the rewards both in time and eternity are well worth the effort. Joseph Smith said: "When you climb up a ladder, you must begin at the bottom, and ascend step by step, until you arrive at the top; and so it is with the principles of the Gospel—you must begin with the first, and go on until you learn all the principles of exaltation. But it will be a great while after you have passed through the veil before you will have learned them. It is not all to be comprehended in this world" (*Teachings of the Prophet Joseph Smith,* sel. Joseph Fielding Smith [Salt Lake City: Deseret Book, 1976], 348).

"I HAVE HAD GREAT JOY IN THEE ALREADY"

As a father, I have been impressed with the manner in which Alma the Younger taught his sons. He understood the need to stop occasionally and see how far one has traveled. Although he did not say as much to his son Shiblon as he did to Helaman and Corianton, a great message is contained in what he did say. Along with his exhortations, Alma focused on the progress of Shiblon and praised him for the qualities he already possessed. "And now, my son, I trust that I shall have great joy in you, because of your steadiness and your faithfulness unto God; for as you have commenced in your youth to look to the Lord your God, even so I hope that you will continue in keeping his commandments. . . . I say unto you, my son, that I have had great joy in thee already, because of thy faithfulness and thy diligence, and thy patience and thy long-suffering among the people of the Zoramites. For I know that thou wast in bonds; yea, and I also know that thou wast stoned for the word's sake; and thou didst bear all these things with patience because the Lord was with thee" (Alma 38:2–4).

How encouraging these words must have been for Shiblon. There were still things his father encouraged him to do, but he enjoyed looking down the mountain for a moment to see how far he had come.

MY HOPE COLLECTION

If I climb with a group, others may climb faster than I do. When I look up the mountain and see them high above me on the trail, I feel a little jolt of despair, so I have learned not to look at others' positions on the trail. When we compare ourselves to others we may lose hope if they are higher on the path than we are, or we may face the battle of pride if we perceive we are higher.

Over the years I have collected a series of quotations from the Brethren that I call my "hope collection." They encourage us to see the positive in ourselves and others without comparing ourselves to anyone else. Following are a few quotations from my collection that will create hope in others' hearts as they have in mine.

Brigham Young

President Brigham Young said: "Thousands of temptations assail, and you make a miss here and a slip there, and say that you have not lived up to all the knowledge you have. True; but often it is a marvel to me that you have lived up to so much as you have, considering the power of the enemy upon the earth. Few that have ever lived have fully understood that power. I do not fully comprehend the awful power and influence Satan has upon the earth, but I understand enough to know that it is a marvel that the Latter-day Saints are as good as they are" (*Journal of Discourses*, 8:285).

On another occasion, while addressing the Saints, Brigham Young spoke on the same theme. "Serve God according to the best knowledge you have, and lay down and sleep quietly; and when the devil comes along and says, 'You are not a very good Saint, you might enjoy greater blessings and more of the power

of God, and have the vision of your mind opened, if you would
live up to your privileges,' tell him to leave; that you have long ago
forsaken his ranks and enlisted in the army of Jesus, who is your
captain, and that you want no more of the Devil" (*Journal of
Discourses*, 4:270).

Discouragement and despair are two of the most effective
tools Lucifer employs, particularly with those for whom perfection of character and obedience is an important goal.

Joseph F. Smith

President Joseph F. Smith told the Saints: "The Lord will
accept that which is enough, with a good deal more pleasure and
satisfaction than that which is too much and unnecessary. It is
good to be earnest, good to be diligent, to persevere, and to be
faithful all the time, but we may go to extremes in these things,
when we do not need to" (*Gospel Doctrine*, 5th ed. [Salt Lake
City: Deseret Book, 1939], 368).

After losing the 116 pages of the Book of Mormon manu-
script, Joseph Smith lost the privilege of translating for a time.
When the gift was restored, the Lord cautioned Joseph lest in his
eagerness to atone for his mistake he push too hard: "See that you
are faithful and continue on unto the finishing of the remainder
of the work of translation as you have begun. Do not run faster or
labor more than you have strength and means provided to enable
you to translate; but be diligent unto the end" (D&C 10:3–4).

I have learned in attempting to conquer various peaks that if
I climb too fast I do not usually cover more ground; I only succeed in exhausting myself.

Heber J. Grant

Heber J. Grant encouraged the Saints, saying: "I do not believe
that any man lives up to his ideals, but if we are striving, if we are

working, if we are trying, to the best of our ability, to improve day by day, then we are in the line of our duty. If we are seeking to remedy our own defects, if we are so living that we can ask God for light, for knowledge, for intelligence, and above all, for His Spirit, that we may overcome our weaknesses, then, I can tell you, we are in the straight and narrow path that leads to life eternal; then we need have no fear" (Conference Report, April 1909, 111).

Ezra Taft Benson

A later generation of Saints was encouraged by President Ezra Taft Benson. He was also concerned that the Saints would become discouraged by their high expectations. "We must be careful, as we seek to become more and more godlike, that we do not become discouraged and lose hope. Becoming Christlike is a lifetime pursuit and very often involves growth and change that is slow, almost imperceptible" (*Teachings of Ezra Taft Benson* [Salt Lake City: Bookcraft, 1988], 72).

When I look down the slope on my climbs, I am often amazed at the distance I have come. It is startling to realize that each tiny step, when added to all the other small steps, produces such heights.

Gordon B. Hinckley

President Gordon B. Hinckley has on numerous occasions reminded us that Jesus was the only perfect man who lived. We are striving to become like him, but we must be patient with each other and ourselves: "None of us is perfect. There was only one perfect man who ever walked the earth, and He was the Son of God. We all have weaknesses and I guess we all make mistakes and will make mistakes in the future, but look for the virtues, the strengths, the goodness in those with whom you labor, and draw those characteristics into your own lives and make them a part of yourselves, and you will be the richer for it all the days that you live" (*Teachings of Gordon B. Hinckley* [Salt Lake City: Deseret Book, 1997], 94).

These statements of the presidents of the Church from many different time periods emphasize that members of the Church from the very beginning of the Restoration have dealt with the same feelings of inadequacy. They too needed to see the progress they had made and allow the effort of the climb to be alleviated by glances back to see how far they had come. They needed hope in their progression.

"HE EMPLOYETH NO SERVANT THERE"

It is also important to realize that the Lord is not trying to make our path difficult. While studying at a large university, I was somewhat distressed when a professor told us he was under pressure to spread out the grades in the class. He needed to have a *B*-average for the class, so he made his tests difficult in order to achieve that desired average.

Jacob spoke of the path one had to travel and of the gate one had to pass through to enter into the Lord's kingdom. I have derived great hope from his words: "O then, my beloved brethren, come unto the Lord, the Holy One. Remember that his paths are righteous. Behold, the way for man is narrow, but it lieth in a straight course before him, and the keeper of the gate is the Holy One of Israel; and he employeth no servant there; and there is none other way save it be by the gate. . . . and whoso knocketh, to him will he open" (2 Nephi 9:41–42).

Jacob teaches that the ways of the Lord are narrow, or strict, but that the path lies in a straight course to the gate. In the ancient world, gates were the weakest part of the defenses of a city. To make it more difficult to get into the city, the gate contained numerous turns. This slowed any attacking forces.

The Lord's paths and gate, however, do not contain turns. The Lord is not trying to keep us out of his city. In fact, he is the gatekeeper, and he is the most merciful gatekeeper there is. Jacob assures us we need only knock and He will open the gate.

"ACCORDING TO THE DESIRE OF THEIR HEARTS"

The Lord tells us there are two things he looks at when he judges our climb toward perfection. "For I, the Lord, will judge all men according to their works, according to the desire of their hearts" (D&C 137:9). We realize that our works still have a great way to go. There are things we do that we wish we didn't; there are things we should do, or do better, with which we still struggle. But the Lord comforts us with the knowledge that our desires also count. Sometimes we need to stop for a moment and look at our desires. For most of us they are much higher than our works. Much of our frustration with ourselves is found in the distance between these two elevations.

The Lord knows we want to be good. He knows we want to do, think, speak, and feel all the right things. He is aware of our desire to be like the Savior. In time our works will, hopefully, catch up with our desires, but for the time being they have not reached the same level. Right now we are closer to the peak in our desires, and the Lord tells us that this is also important. If at the Judgment, the Lord will throw into his eternal scale our desires, surely, that will tip them in our favor.

"BLESSED ARE THEY WHICH DO HUNGER AND THIRST AFTER RIGHTEOUSNESS"

The Beatitude that touches me the most and instills hope in my heart is the fourth one. It states, "Blessed are they which do hunger and thirst after righteousness: for they shall be filled" (Matthew 5:6). In the Book of Mormon we learn "they shall be filled with the Holy Ghost" (3 Nephi 12:6). Most Latter-day Saints truly do hunger after righteousness. They deeply desire to live up to every expectation of the Lord. They want this degree of integrity and devotion as much as they want food and water. The Lord did not say, "Blessed are they who have achieved righteousness," but rather, "blessed are they which do hunger and thirst" after it. The desire alone is not sufficient, but the desire alone is worthy of the word *blessed*. The Holy Ghost is given as a gift to help the individual achieve a state of ultimate righteousness.

"THE CLEARER ARE HIS VIEWS"

During my climbs, when I saw the peak a compelling desire was created within me to reach my goal. I believe that is also true of our spiritual efforts. Joseph Smith taught: "We consider that God has created man with a mind capable of instruction, and a faculty which may be enlarged in proportion to the heed and diligence given to the light communicated from heaven to the intellect; and that the nearer man approaches perfection, the clearer are his views, and the greater his enjoyments, till he has overcome the evils of his life and lost every desire for sin; and like the ancients, arrives at that point of faith where he is wrapped in the power and glory of his Maker and is caught up to dwell with Him. But we consider that this is a station to which no man ever arrived in a moment: he must have been instructed in the government and laws of that kingdom by proper degrees, until his mind is capable in some measure of comprehending the propriety, justice, equality, and consistency of the same" (*Teachings of the Prophet Joseph Smith,* 51).

There is tremendous hope in knowing that the higher we climb, the less pull the forces of the world have on us. Our initial efforts may seem to us laborious, and we may fear they will always be as difficult. The adversary will try to convince us that the climb gets increasingly difficult. But Joseph Smith assures us that the nearer to perfection we reach, the clearer our views become and the greater our enjoyments. The fruits of the gospel strengthen and encourage us. It is important to realize this truth lest we become discouraged and give up.

I recall hiking a very muddy canyon in southern Utah. Each new hole we had to cross increased our discouragement. One by one, various members of our group turned back. When we reached a particularly deep hole, one of the hikers said, "Around every bend is another hole. It's not worth it." A few of us pushed through that hole, and it was the last mud we saw. During the rest of the hike we were blessed with spectacular scenery.

Joseph Smith indicated perfection was something we do not arrive at "in a moment" but "by proper degrees." Even Jesus needed to grow in this manner. Often, when the Lord wished to emphasize something in the scriptures he repeated it several times. Notice the emphasis the Lord gives in Doctrine and Covenants 93 to the truth stated by Joseph Smith as it relates to the Savior: "And I, John, saw that he received not of the fullness at the first, but received grace for grace; and he received not of the fulness at first, but continued from grace to grace, until he received a fullness; and thus he was called the Son of God, because he received not of the fullness at the first" (vv. 12–14). We are encouraged to follow in the Savior's footsteps. "I give unto you these sayings that you may understand and know how to worship, and know what you worship, that you may come unto the Father in my name, and in due time receive of his fulness. . . . Therefore, I say unto you, you shall receive grace for grace" (vv. 19–20).

RETURN AND TIDY UP

We might compare overcoming the natural man to cleaning up an untidy room. Each of us is blessed with the light of Christ.

The Lord asks us to enter the room of our soul with this light in hand and to tidy it up. Once inside, we notice that the furniture is out of place, books are scattered on the floor, and the lamp is knocked down. We right the lamp, replace the books, and straighten the couch and chair. We hold our light up and say, "Everything looks tidy and clean."

The Lord responds by saying, "Here is a greater light. Return to the room of your soul and tidy up again." With the Lord's gift of greater light, we return and look around. We now see things we did not notice before. The rug in the middle of the room is not centered, and some of the books are upside down. The lamp shade is tilted, and the couch cushions are backwards. We take care of all these things, look around again, and say, "Everything looks tidy and clean."

Our reward for these efforts is more light. "That which is of God is light; and he that receiveth light, and continueth in God, receiveth more light; and that light groweth brighter and brighter until the perfect day" (D&C 50:24). The Lord once again asks us to return and tidy up. In this brighter light, we can now see things we did not notice before. The furniture needs dusting and the floor sweeping. We dust and sweep and say, "Everything looks tidy and clean."

Our obedience brings more commandments, more light. "Blessed are they . . . who have obeyed my gospel; for they shall receive for their reward . . . commandments not a few, and . . . revelations in their time—they that are faithful and diligent before me" (D&C 59:3-4). We return to the room of our soul. Now we notice the tiny cobwebs in the corners and the dulled sheen on the surface of the furniture. We remove the cobwebs and polish the furniture. This process continues throughout life.

The more we progress toward perfection, the more the Lord reveals the weaknesses in our character. But all the time our character is becoming more refined and more like the Savior's. Hope is kept alive by the realization that we are responding to the Lord's light, and we are growing grace for grace.

SPRING COMES LATE

When I get discouraged with this constant cleaning process, I sometimes climb mountains. The physical progression of movement up a mountain is very refreshing and never fails to instill in me hope for spiritual progression.

Feeling a little dispirited one day, I took a hike in the Rocky Mountains of southern Alberta. I was not very hopeful about my progress toward perfection, and my weaknesses lay heavy in my heart. It was late spring in the valley. The flowers were out, the trees full of leaves, and warm breezes were blowing. The higher I climbed, the less green I saw. Snow lay in patches on the trail. After a few hours of climbing, I saw very few signs of spring. All around it was still cold, still winter.

I sat down on a rock to rest and began to ponder and pray. I noticed a little bush in front of me; it had tiny green buds on it— just the promise of spring. As I stared at it, the little plant seemed to whisper these words, "In the highest mountains, spring comes late." I wondered what those words meant until I had studied the green buds long enough to realize that our lives can be much like that little bush.

We'll never be content with the valley and the spring that comes early at the foot of the mountain. We want the peaks. On the celestial mountaintop, spring comes late, but our lives will show green buds that promise the eternal spring that will one day come if we keep hope alive.

A FORMULA FOR PERFECTION

The Book of Mormon closes with Moroni's formula for perfection. Every time I read it, my hope for eventual perfection is renewed. "I would exhort you that ye would come unto Christ, and lay hold upon every good gift, and touch not the evil gift, nor the unclean thing. . . . Yea, come unto Christ, and be perfected in him, and deny yourselves of all ungodliness; and if ye shall deny yourselves of all ungodliness, and love God with all your might, mind and strength, then is his grace sufficient for you, that by his grace ye may be perfect in Christ . . . that ye become holy, without spot" (Moroni 10:30, 32–33).

The Lord asks us to do four things: First, come unto Christ—that is, have faith in him and his atonement. Second, lay hold upon every good thing in life, in other words, truly strive to live the thirteenth Article of Faith. Third, shun every evil, unclean, or ungodly thing. Fourth, love God with all our heart and soul. If our lives reflect these four efforts, we are promised that his grace is sufficient and he will make us perfect.

It is not necessary to attain perfection by ourselves; indeed, it is impossible to do so. Nephi testified that "it is by grace that we are saved, after all we can do" (2 Nephi 25:23). I do not think that means we do all we can and he will do the rest; rather, I think it means that even if we do everything that is asked of us, we will still need his grace. Our hope lies in his willingness to grant it.

The celestial kingdom is described as containing "just men made perfect through Jesus the mediator of the new covenant, who wrought out this perfect atonement through the shedding of his own blood" (D&C 76:69). Jesus is our mediator, our advocate, our defense attorney; when he pleads for us, it is not our perfection he lays before the Father as evidence that we merit exaltation; rather, it is his own supreme sacrifice. After we've presented our temple recommend, our tithing receipts, our home teaching records, our mission release, and our family history as evidence, the Savior presents the most convincing argument in our behalf.

"Listen to him who is the advocate with the Father, who is

pleading your cause before him—Saying: Father, behold the sufferings and death of him who did no sin, in whom thou wast well pleased; behold the blood of thy Son which was shed, the blood of him whom thou gavest that thyself might be glorified; Wherefore, Father, spare these my brethren that believe on my name, that they may come unto me and have everlasting life" (D&C 45:3-5).

THE MAN IN THE LAST CHAIR

I sometimes picture the Judgment as a large waiting room with chairs against the walls like those in a doctor's office. Each chair is filled with a man, and each one is a Mike Wilcox. A door opens and a messenger points to the first man and says, "Will Mike Wilcox, the husband of Laura Wilcox, please step forward and render an account of his stewardship." The first man rises and enters the room and does not return. Later the messenger returns, points to the second chair and states, "Would Mike Wilcox, the father of Kirsten Wilcox, please step forward and render an account of his stewardship." The second man rises, enters the judgment hall, and does not return.

When their turns come, the third, fourth, fifth and sixth Mike Wilcoxes go into the hall. They are the fathers of Megan, Benjamin, Cade, and Mckay Wilcox. The door opens once again and the messenger calls out, "Would Mike Wilcox the son and descendant, come forward and render an account of his stewardship." The man in the seventh chair rises and reports.

The man in the eighth chair is next called. This man is Mike Wilcox the teacher. He must render an account of how he used the opportunities and talents he was given.

I don't know what men sit in the other chairs, but I am sure of who is sitting in the last chair. He is very uncomfortable and nervous. Nephi's words, "O wretched man that I am" (2 Nephi 4:17), might be an apt description of this last man.

The door opens for the last time and the messenger appears, saying, "Will Mike Wilcox, the man, please come forward and render an account of his character." Now the very core of who I am will be examined. I know this man very well. He is not perfect. He is often impatient. He has not yet conquered envy, pride, or the tendency to judge others. He has not mastered selflessness or complete control of thoughts, words, and feelings. He sometimes serves more out of a sense of duty than love.

The man in the last chair rises and moves slowly toward the judgment hall. At that moment another person enters the room and stands by his side. His voice is calm and assured. "Do not be afraid to go before my Father," he says. "I will go with you and plead for you, because you have always loved me and believed on my name." The sweetest peace of hope is then born in the man's heart as together they go before the Father.

None of us, no matter how righteous we are, no matter how high we have climbed, will ever take the final steps to the peak alone. Another will take them with us: the only One who could conquer the peak alone, the first master of the mountain. Having reached the peak, he returns to help us up so that together we might enjoy the view.

CHAPTER SIX

We glory in tribulations also:
knowing that tribulation worketh patience;
and patience, experience;
and experience, hope:
and hope maketh not ashamed.

−ROMANS 5:3-5

HOPE TO ENDURE TRIALS

One of the first truths we are taught about our experiences here on earth is the inevitability of trials. We will face not only temptations from the adversary but also the trials that naturally arise with mortality. They come from different sources and vary in their intensity. Some are self-created, flowing from the normal consequences of our own weaknesses; some stem from the actions of others; and some are designed by a wise Heavenly Father to serve as a refiner's fire, purging out the dross of our characters. They are physical, spiritual, emotional, and mental in nature and every combination of these. They are part of the opposition of life so eloquently explained by Lehi to his son Jacob in 2 Nephi 2.

Often when we experience these trials, hope wavers and we feel defenseless. We may feel like the wives and children Jacob spoke of when he said, "Many hearts died, pierced with deep wounds" (Jacob 2:35). A friend of mine undergoing a deep sorrow expressed to me the belief that he would never be happy again. He was convinced that true joy had vanished from his life. Although he could function in his responsibilities and callings, a light had been extinguished from his life—the light of hope. Many months later he related to me the following experience.

"I did not wish to remain in a state of grief, so I tried very hard not to think of the reason for my sorrow, but even if I could put it entirely out of my mind, the very effort would be a reminder, and I would lapse back into melancholy. Then one day I was walking on Temple Square. It was in the spring, and the flowers and shrubbery were beautiful. A breeze was blowing, the air was fresh, and sparrows were chattering in a nearby tree.

"I know this all sounds very clichéd, but I found myself standing in a patch of sunlight that filtered through the trees. I walked slowly for just a moment to enjoy my surroundings and realized the emotion of happiness and peace was in my heart. I had not felt it for such a long time that I stopped and said right out loud, 'I am feeling joy!'

"When I said this, I remembered why I had not felt happy for such a long time, and the haze of sorrow I had lived in for the past year returned. But I was a different man. Hope had been reborn in that little patch of sunlight. I began to weep, but they were tears of relief. I knew if I could feel joy for just a minute, the time would come when I would feel it for an hour, and then a day, a week, and even years."

Like my friend we need little patches of sunlight amidst the clouds. If we turn to the scriptures, the Lord will teach us how to find those patches and endure through hope the pain we may be called upon to bear.

THE FOURTH WATCH PRINCIPLE

The evening that Jesus fed the five thousand, he sent the apostles to the Sea of Galilee, instructing them "to go to the other side before unto Bethsaida, while he sent away the people. . . . And when even was come, the ship was in the midst of the sea, and he alone on the land. And he saw them toiling in rowing; for the wind was contrary unto them and about the fourth watch of the night he cometh unto them, walking upon the sea. . . . They all saw him, and were troubled. And immediately he talked with them, and saith unto them, Be of good cheer: it is I; be not afraid. And he went up unto them into the ship; and the wind ceased" (Mark 6:45–51).

John's account of this same event tells us that "the sea arose by reason of a great wind that blew. So when they had rowed about five and twenty or thirty furlongs, they see Jesus walking on the sea" (John 6:18–19). (Thirty furlongs is the equivalent of about sixty-five to seventy football fields). Matthew's account assures us they were "tossed with waves" (Matthew 14:24).

Undoubtedly they were exhausted not only because they had rowed such a great distance against the wind but also because of the time. The Jews divided the night into four watches. The first watch lasted from six in the evening to nine, the second from nine to midnight, the third from midnight to three in the morning, and the fourth from three to six in the morning. They had been rowing from late afternoon until early in the morning; some of the time they had rowed into a storm.

I cannot help but wonder if they did not wish the Lord had been with them. They had already seen him calm a storm and take them safely to shore. Although he was not with them in the ship, Mark assures us "he saw them toiling in rowing." They could not have known that their danger and their efforts were being watched by their Lord as he stood on the hills overlooking the Sea of Galilee.

There are times in all of our lives when the wind is contrary to us and we toil in rowing. We look at the waves around us and feel isolated in the midst of our stormy sea of trial. We cling to our anchor of hope, knowing there is One who is aware of our danger, who watches from his high vantage point, and who will come to us.

HER FATHER WAS THERE ALL THE TIME

In Southern California one winter, I went down to the ocean for a walk. There were cliffs overlooking the beach, and I walked along the edge, enjoying the sea. I looked down at the beach below and saw a small girl about six or seven years old dancing and skipping along the shore. She would run toward the surf and then retreat as it raced toward her. Occasionally she would stop, pick up a intriguing shell or stone, and then throw it into the waves. She was having such fun, and it was heartening to watch her enjoy her carefree morning.

Yet I was fearful for an unaccompanied young child on an abandoned beach. I decided to watch until someone came for her or she left to return home. When she reached a spot directly below me, she turned with a big smile, looked to the top of the cliffs, and waved. At first I thought she was waving at me, but her eyes were directed to my left. I turned and saw her father. He waved back, and she continued down the beach.

Her father had been walking along the top of the cliff, keeping his eye on his daughter. He passed by me, staying abreast of his child, and continued down to the shore. So, too, does our Father in Heaven watch us, even though at times we are unaware that his solicitous eyes are upon us.

"BE OF GOOD CHEER: IT IS I"

The Savior came to his disciples in the fourth watch. I am sure they would have welcomed him in the first. When our boat is tossed in the waves, when we are exhausted from rowing and fearful of capsizing, we desire the Lord to come to us immediately.

When he does not appear in the first watch, surely he will come in the second, we say to ourselves. By the third watch we may doubt not only our own strength to endure but also his love. We must not abandon hope. Remember, he is on the mountain watching us and knows our strength to endure better than we do. In the fourth watch he will come, and we will hear those comforting words, "Be of good cheer: it is I; be not afraid." In his wisdom he knows that our own efforts, even though they may appear futile against the strength of the winds, are necessary for our growth.

While struggling with the adversary in the Sacred Grove, Joseph reached "the fourth watch" before he saw the pillar of light that released him from his trauma. Joseph teaches us an important truth as he describes the darkness of that moment. "But, exerting all my powers to call upon God to deliver me out of the power of this enemy which had seized upon me, and at the very moment when I was ready to sink into despair and abandon myself to destruction. . . . Just at this moment of great alarm, I saw a pillar of light" (Joseph Smith–History 1:16). If the Savior has not come to us in our hour of need, we must not believe that he does not care or that he is unaware. We must conclude that we have not yet reached the "moment of great alarm"; we have not rowed until the fourth watch, for he will never let us reach that moment and not come to our aid.

In Liberty Jail, where Joseph Smith faced one of the severest trials of his life, he wrote a letter to the Saints wherein he compared the trials of the Church to a ship tossed in a storm. He then counseled, "Therefore, dearly beloved brethren, let us cheerfully do all things that lie in our power; and then may we stand still, with the utmost assurance, to see the salvation of God, and for his arm to be revealed" (D&C 123:17).

"I PREPARE YOU AGAINST THESE THINGS"

What if we reach the fourth watch and still he does not appear? If we find ourselves in this situation, the story of the Jaredites will supply us with the hope to endure.

When the brother of Jared arrived at the seashore with his small band, the Lord commanded him to make barges to carry his people across the ocean to the promised land. The eight barges were "tight like unto a dish" (Ether 2:17). That was true of the bottom, top, sides, and door. After having constructed the barges according to the instructions of the Lord, the brother of Jared had two problems. There was neither air nor light within the watertight vessels. The Lord solved the air problem but left the light problem to the brother of Jared:

"What will ye that I should do that ye may have light in your vessels? . . . For behold, ye shall be as a whale in the midst of the sea; for the mountain waves shall dash upon you. Nevertheless, I will bring you up again out of the depths of the sea; for the winds have gone forth out of my mouth, and also the rains and the floods have I sent forth" (Ether 2:23-24).

When the Jaredites departed in their barges, we are told, "the Lord God caused that there should be a furious wind blow upon the face of the waters, towards the promised land; and thus they were tossed upon the waves of the sea before the wind. And it came to pass that they were many times buried in the depths of the sea, because of the mountain waves which broke upon them, and also the great and terrible tempests which were caused by the fierceness of the wind" (Ether 6:5-6).

I have tried to put myself in the place of the brother of Jared. I wonder if I would not have said to the Lord: "Since the winds proceed from thy mouth and the waves are controlled by thee, why not quiet the storms for us while we cross? Blow more gently, and we won't need these 'tight like a dish' boats at all. We can stay out on deck, enjoy the sunshine, catch fish, and in general have a pleasant voyage to America."

We know from other scriptures that the Lord can still the storms of nature. I have wondered if a similar thought crossed the brother of Jared's mind for he said: "O Lord, thou has said we must be encompassed about by the floods" (Ether 3:2). In other words, since this is the way it must be, we will accept thy wisdom.

In our own lives the winds blow, the mountain waves crash, and the tempests rage. During such times in my life, I always hope the Lord will still the storms and give me a gentle voyage, but often the winds still blow. If we feel we have reached the fourth watch, the moment of great alarm, and the Lord does not come to us, we must not assume he does not care or we are unworthy of his attention. There is still a source of hope to which we can hold. Notice the words of the Lord to the brother of Jared:

"And behold, I prepare you against these things; for ye cannot cross this great deep save I prepare you against the waves of the sea, and the winds which have gone forth, and the floods which shall come. Therefore what will ye that I should prepare you that ye may have light when ye are swallowed up in the depths of the sea?" (Ether 2:25).

In his foreknowledge and wisdom, the Lord will prepare us for the winds and waves that will come into our lives. He knows trials will test us, and he will see to it that the preparations are made to enable us to withstand them. We may not be aware of his preparations, but we must have confidence, assured that our vessels are "tight like a dish." If they are not, he will either still the storm or come to us in the "fourth watch." Perhaps Isaiah was thinking of that principle when he said, "And it shall come to pass, that before they call, I will answer" (Isaiah 65:24).

THE LION AND THE BEAR

When David faced Goliath, he was confident that he could succeed. What was the foundation for this hope? Earlier experiences had prepared him for his present challenge. "And David said unto Saul, Thy servant kept his father's sheep, and there came a lion, and a bear, and took a lamb out of the flock: And I went out after him, and smote him. . . . Thy servant slew both the lion and the bear; and this uncircumcised Philistine shall be as one of them. . . . The Lord that delivered me out of the paw of the lion, and out of the paw of the bear, he will deliver me out of the hand of this Philistine" (1 Samuel 17:34–37).

David's experiences with the lion and the bear were part of the Lord's preparing him for a greater enemy. The courage to face Goliath was forged in the heat of previous conflicts. If we are asked to face a Goliath, we will previously have faced and conquered a lion and a bear. The Lord would not leave us to face trials if he did not know that we had been prepared to come off victorious.

"FRUITFUL IN THE LAND OF . . . AFFLICTION"

The scriptures teach us other principles of hope to which we may cling during times of trial and sorrow. In every book of scripture we are taught that the Lord will make all things good for us if we will continue to live righteously and trust in him.

When Joseph was sold into Egypt, he had every reason to feel life was unfair. Imprisoned for his virtuous stand against temptation, Joseph explained, "Indeed I was stolen away out of the land of the Hebrews: and here also have I done nothing that they should put me into the dungeon" (Genesis 40:15). Yet Joseph was not abandoned. We are specifically told "the Lord was with him" (Genesis 39:2, 23).

After many years, Joseph finally stood before Pharaoh,

interpreted his dreams and was raised to a position of authority. Two sons were born to him and his wife, Asenath. The names Joseph chose for his two sons teach us that the Lord can make even the worst of situations positive if, like Joseph, we trust him and are patient.

"And Joseph called the name of the firstborn Manasseh: for God, said he, hath made me forget all my toil, and all my father's house. And the name of the second called he Ephraim: for God hath caused me to be fruitful in the land of my affliction" (Genesis 41:51–52).

Part of the Lord's greatness is his ability to bless us in such a way that we forget the pains and toil of the past in the realization that we can be fruitful even in affliction. Because Joseph realized this truth, he was able to comfort his brothers when he revealed his identity to them. "Now therefore be not grieved, nor angry with yourselves, that ye sold me hither: for God did send me before you to preserve life. . . . So now it was not you that sent me hither, but God" (Genesis 45:5, 8). Years later, when their father, Jacob, died, and the brothers believed Joseph would now take his revenge, he once again reassured them by testifying to them that the Lord can turn all trials to blessings. "But as for you, ye thought evil against me; but God meant it unto good, to bring to pass, as it is this day, to save much people alive" (Genesis 50:20).

"THOU KNOWEST THE GREATNESS OF GOD"

The Lord so desires us to believe he can make all experiences of life positive that he repeats this lesson throughout the scriptures. Just before his death, Lehi testified of this principle to his son Jacob, who in his "childhood" had "suffered afflictions and much sorrow because of the rudeness of [his] brethren. "Nevertheless, Jacob, my firstborn in the wilderness, Thou knowest the greatness of God; and he shall consecrate thine afflictions for thy gain. Wherefore, thy soul shall be blessed" (2 Nephi 2:1–3). Even the afflictions of childhood can be turned to good in the wisdom of the Lord.

Joseph Smith was told early in his ministry to "be patient in afflictions, for thou shalt have many; but endure them, for, lo, I am with thee, even unto the end of thy days" (D&C 24:8). Perhaps none of his many afflictions struck him so deeply as his months in Liberty Jail. There, however, he learned that "walls and irons, doors and creaking hinges, and half-scared-to-death guards and jailers . . . are calculated in their very nature to make the soul of an honest man feel stronger than the powers of hell" (*Teachings of the Prophet Joseph Smith,* sel. Joseph Fielding Smith [Salt Lake City: Deseret Book, 1976], 139). During these days of learning Joseph was assured "all these things shall give thee experience, and shall be for thy good. . . . Therefore, hold on thy way" (D&C 122:7, 9).

In his letter to the Corinthians, the apostle Paul detailed some of his sufferings for the cause of Christ (2 Corinthians 11:24–28). Yet he bore a powerful testimony to the Roman Saints that he knew "that all things work together for good to them that love God" (Romans 8:28). As long as we believe the testimonies of Joseph, Lehi, Joseph Smith, Paul, and many others, hope in trial will never die. The day will come when we will realize the Lord has turned trials to blessings.

POOLS OF WATER IN THE DESERT

I have long found comfort in the words of C. S. Lewis, whose own experiences with life taught him of the greatness of God:

"Ye cannot in your present state understand eternity. . . . But ye can get some likeness of it if ye say that both good and evil, when they are full grown, become retrospective. . . . All this earthly past will have been Heaven to those who are saved. . . . All their life on earth too, will then be seen by the damned to have been Hell. That is what mortals misunderstand. They say of some temporal suffering, 'No future bliss can make up for it,' not knowing that Heaven, once attained, will work backwards and turn even that agony into a glory. And of some sinful pleasure they say 'Let me but have *this* and I'll take the consequences': little dreaming how damnation will spread back and back into their past and contaminate the pleasure of the sin. Both processes begin even before death. The good man's past begins to change so that his forgiven sins and remembered sorrows take on the quality of Heaven: the bad man's past already conforms to his badness and is filled only with dreariness. And that is why, at the end of all things, when the sun rises here and the twilight turns to blackness down there, the Blessed will say, 'We have never lived anywhere except in Heaven,' and the Lost, 'We were always in Hell.' And both will speak truly. . . .

"Ah, the Saved . . . what happens to them is best described as the opposite of a mirage. What seemed, when they entered it, to be the vale of misery, turns out, when they look back, to have been a well; and where present experience saw only salt deserts, memory truthfully records that the pools were full of water" (*The Great Divorce* [New York: Macmillan, 1977], 67–68).

"GOD SHALL WIPE AWAY ALL TEARS"

There is a promise recorded three times in the Bible, once in Isaiah, and twice in the book of Revelation, that imparts great hope to any who have walked the paths of sorrow. Speaking of the Savior, Isaiah prophesied, "He will swallow up death in victory; and the Lord God will wipe away tears from off all faces" (Isaiah 25:8). In Revelation the Lord promises that he will come to us in our sorrows and wipe away our tears: "For the Lamb . . . shall feed them, and shall lead them unto living fountains of

waters: and God shall wipe away all tears from their eyes"
(Revelation 7:17). This was such an important source of hope that
John repeated these comforting words, adding details to them, at
the end of Revelation: "And God shall wipe away all tears from
their eyes; and there shall be no more death, neither sorrow, nor
crying, neither shall there be any more pain: for the former things
are passed away" (Revelation 21:4).

When I served as a bishop, I saw many tears. I kept tissues
nearby, because on any given Sunday, I knew I would use them. I
saw tears of men, women, and children. I saw tears of sorrow over
the death of beloved children who returned to their Father in
Heaven in tragic ways. I saw tears of anguish over straying or
rebellious children who were dying spiritually. I saw tears of grief
over inactive husbands, tears of pain brought on by divorce or
unfaithfulness. I saw tears that came from old, tired bodies longing for the grave and reunion with loved ones beyond the veil.
Perhaps most painful of all were the tears of guilt and bitter sorrow due to broken commandments.

Each time I listened to their sorrows, I would hand them a tissue. They would wipe the tears away, but I was often troubled by
my inability to provide more comfort, to find the words that
would turn pain to joy. During one of those troubled moments I
read the words of the Lord in Isaiah and Revelation. Though I was
not capable of wiping the tears away, there was One who could,
One who promised he would wipe "all tears" from off "all faces."

Jesus has many titles that are introduced and repeated
throughout the scriptures. The one I love best is "I am Alpha and
Omega, the beginning and the end" (Revelation 21:6). What is
Jesus the end of? What is he the beginning of? He is the end of
crying. He is the end of death. He is the end of sorrow. He is the
end of pain. He is the end of guilt. He is the end of tears of sorrow. By contrast, he is the beginning of life. He is the beginning

of happiness. He is the beginning of peace. He is the beginning of mercy. He is the beginning of joy.

There is such hope in the words, "God shall wipe away all tears from their eyes." The promise is that the Savior will wipe the tears away, not merely hand us a tissue. There is the suggestion of a very intimate and familial relationship in the Lord's promise. I would not presume to wipe the tears from the eyes of anyone with whom I was not intimately acquainted. I have watched my wife gently wipe the tears from the cheeks of our children. It is a gesture of love and tenderness, a gesture of the Savior himself, a gesture of hope.

"IT IS FINISHED"

While on the cross, denied even the comfort of a drink of water in his thirst, the Savior cried out to his Father in Heaven. No mortal being ever suffered more than he did. No grief was greater, no sorrow darker, no pain more intense. Yet, there came a time when the supreme sacrifice was completed, and Jesus said, "It is finished" (John 19:30). He had fulfilled his Father's will to the last biting taste of vinegar on his lips. But "It is finished" was also true of his pain. The agony, the betrayal, the grief of Gethsemane and the thorns of Calvary were over.

One great source of hope is the assurance that no matter what pain, sorrow, or grief we bear, no matter what trial still hangs heavy in our hearts, all of us will one day be able to say, "It is finished." There is an end to suffering. Jesus is that end. There is a beginning to joy. In Christ we find that hope-filled beginning.

"YE SHALL ONE DAY REST FROM ALL YOUR AFFLICTIONS"

Amulek suffered great sorrow. He witnessed the death by fire of the women and children of his hometown of Ammonihah. His own wife and children may have been among the martyrs. He was imprisoned, beaten, and mocked "for many days" (Alma 14:22). He was "rejected by those who were once his friends and also by his father and his kindred" (Alma 15:16). In light of his past experiences, his words of comfort to the suffering Zoramite poor have greater weight: "Have patience, and bear with those afflictions, with a firm hope that ye shall one day rest from all your afflictions" (Alma 34:41). I am sure that Amulek still felt sorrow when he reflected on the scenes of his past in Ammonihah, but he had a firm hope that the day would come when even the painful memories would fade in the rest the Lord prepares for those who serve and love him.

CHAPTER SEVEN

If in this life only
we have hope in Christ,
we are of all men most miserable.

−1 CORINTHIANS 15:19

HOPE FOR
A BETTER WORLD

When I was a teenager, I picked up a magazine in one of my classes. An article about a fierce civil war raging in a far-off area of the world was accompanied by vivid pictures of the fighting and destruction. I had seen such pictures many times, but none struck me so forcefully as a picture of a young refugee mother and her child. They were staring blankly into the camera. There was no life in their expressions—no emotion, not even fear, just a look of complete hopelessness. To this day I can see the deadness of those eyes and think about what took the light out of them. Perhaps that is what the Lord meant when, speaking of the last days, he said, "Men's hearts shall fail them" (D&C 45:26).

Sometimes the world around us presents a bleak picture. Most news today is negative, chronicling scene after scene of war, crime, disaster, corruption, dishonesty, poverty, and disease. If we are not careful we may become cynical, despondent, or hopeless. We live in a world where evil appears at times to be winning, a world that is slipping deeper and deeper into the fulness of iniquity. The Lord described our world in this way: "For all flesh is corrupted before me; and the powers of darkness prevail upon the earth, among the children of men, in the presence of all the hosts of heaven—Which causeth silence to reign, and all eternity is pained, and the angels are waiting the great command to reap down the earth, to gather the tares that they may be burned; and, behold, the enemy is combined" (D&C 38:11-12). This description was given in 1831, and it is even more certainly true now.

"I SHALL BE LIFTED UP AT THE LAST DAY"

The Book of Mormon was written specifically for our times. Its principal abridgers, Mormon and Moroni, lived in a world that in many ways reflects our own. Yet Mormon and Moroni both spoke consistently of hope. Their lives were filled with scenes of sorrow and destruction. Mormon wrote: "Upon these plates I did forbear to make a full account of their wickedness and abominations, for behold, a continual scene of wickedness and abominations has been before mine eyes ever since I have been sufficient to behold the ways of man. And woe is me because of their wickedness; for my heart has been filled with sorrow because of their wickedness, all my days; nevertheless, I know that I shall be lifted up at the last day" (Mormon 2:18-19).

Mormon found hope in a future world of peace and rest. Knowing that his son Moroni was also filled with sorrow over the terrible scenes he witnessed, he directed his attention to a better world that awaited them both. At the conclusion of a letter that detailed the horrible sufferings of his people, Mormon wrote: "My son, be faithful in Christ; and may not the things which I have written grieve thee, to weigh thee down unto death; but may Christ lift thee up, and may his sufferings and death, and the showing of his body unto our fathers, and his mercy and long-suffering, and the hope of his glory and of eternal life, rest in your mind forever" (Moroni 9:25). In spite of living in a world of darkness, they shared the hope of a world of glory and eternal life.

LAY HOLD UPON EVERY GOOD THING

Moroni was not the only person Mormon tried to comfort by directing his mind to a place of rest. He addressed the believing Nephites, offering them hope for both this world and the next: "I would speak unto you that are of the church, that are the peaceable followers of Christ, and that have obtained a sufficient hope by which ye can enter into the rest of the Lord, from this time henceforth until ye shall rest with him in heaven" (Moroni 7:3).

While waiting to obtain the rest of heaven, Mormon knew people needed hope for their day-to-day lives. He therefore gave them something positive to search for, knowing it would keep hope alive. In their world of incessant evil, Mormon encouraged Church members to "lay hold upon every good thing" they could find. He repeated this counsel numerous times while addressing his people. Not only were they to lay hold upon every good thing but they were to "cleave" unto it once they found it (Moroni 7:25, 28). These good things would be revealed to them if they would "search diligently in the light of Christ" (Moroni 7:19).

Even in the most evil of environments, there is still goodness if we search for it. Today, we are encouraged to seek things that are virtuous, lovely, praiseworthy, and of good report. Seeking these things in a troubled world produces hope. Mormon knew that and turned his people's attention to searching for good. The hope created by their search would be increased by the calm assurance of eternal life that awaited those who kept their faith and persevered in cleaving to good.

"And again, my beloved brethren, I would speak unto you concerning hope. How is it that ye can attain unto faith, save ye shall have hope? And what is it that ye shall hope for? Behold I say unto you that ye shall have hope through the atonement of Christ and the power of his resurrection, to be raised unto life eternal, and this because of your faith in him according to the promise" (Moroni 7:40–41).

"A MORE EXCELLENT HOPE"

After the last great battle between the Nephites and the Lamanites, Moroni, alone, and hiding from the Lamanites, began to abridge the Jaredite records. His attention was captured by the words of Ether regarding hope, and he included them in his abridgement. Once again the focus of his words centered on a world beyond mortality. "Wherefore, whoso believeth in God might with surety hope for a better world, yea, even a place at the right hand of God, which hope cometh of faith, maketh an anchor to the souls of men, which would make them sure and steadfast, always abounding in good works, being led to glorify God" (Ether 12:4).

Without that anchor of hope, those who "were once a delightsome people" with "Christ for their shepherd" being "led even by God the Father" could reach the depths of evil that precipitated the Nephite destruction. Mormon lamented, "They are led about by Satan, even as chaff is driven before the wind, or as a vessel is tossed about upon the waves, without sail or anchor, or without anything wherewith to steer her; and even as she is, so are they" (Mormon 5:17–18).

With Ether's words comparing hope to an anchor fresh in his mind, Moroni added his own testimony, one which must have sustained him in his loneliness: "And I also remember that thou hast said that thou hast prepared a house for man, yea, even among the mansions of thy Father, in which man might have a more excellent hope; wherefore man must hope, or he cannot receive an inheritance in the place which thou hast prepared" (Ether 12:32).

Moroni seems to be telling us that only a hope in receiving an inheritance in the mansions of the Father can sustain a life that will "always abound in good works." This idea surely was planted in Moroni's heart by his father, who once wrote to him: "Because of meekness and lowliness of heart cometh the visitation of the Holy Ghost, which Comforter filleth with hope and perfect love, which love endureth by diligence unto prayer, until the end shall come, when all the saints shall dwell with God" (Moroni 8:26).

Jesus also encouraged his apostles during the Last Supper, when he perceived their sorrows and fears, with the thought of an inheritance in one of the mansions of his Father: "Let not your heart be troubled: ye believe in God, believe also in me. In my Father's house are many mansions: if it were not so, I would have told you. I go to prepare a place for you. And if I go and prepare a place for you, I will come again, and receive you unto myself; that where I am, there ye may be also" (John 14:1–3).

The words "many mansions" suggest there is room enough for all. The Savior does not do anything without a purpose, and the truth that he has gone to prepare a place for us assures us he will return to get us and take us to the place he has prepared—a place far different from the world in which we now find ourselves.

"A BETTER COUNTRY"

One blessing of the restored gospel is our great knowledge of the better world of which Mormon and Ether spoke and of the mansions, spoken of by both Moroni and Jesus, that make up that better world. It is a world spoken of numerous times in the scriptures. Paul indicated that Abraham and Sarah, who also lived in a very evil world, desired "a better country, that is, an heavenly:

wherefore God is not ashamed to be called their God: for he hath prepared for them a city" (Hebrews 11:16).

Early in the Restoration, the Lord counseled Emma Smith to "lay aside the things of this world, and seek for the things of a better" (D&C 25:10). Indeed, we are told that "all holy men" sought for a better world and "found it not because of wickedness and abominations; and confessed they were strangers and pilgrims on the earth; but obtained a promise that they should find it and see it in their flesh" (D&C 45:12-14).

THE BETTER WORLD: A WORLD OF LOVE

Hope has ever been associated with charity, the pure love of Christ. Paul indicated that charity was the greatest of all the gifts of God, adding the assurance that it "never faileth" (1 Corinthians 13:8; see also v. 13). Because we are eternal beings who once lived in a world of charity with our Father in Heaven, our present condition presents a challenge indeed. It is little wonder that we long for the love of that lost world and despair when we see it fading.

Although our present world is often described as a place where "the love of men . . . wax[es] cold" (Joseph Smith-Matthew 1:30) and where "they are without affection, and they hate their own blood" (Moses 7:33), the better world we are striving to obtain is a world of charity, a world of love. There, we not only receive love, we give it.

Nephi spoke of two images that represented the love of God: the "fountain of living waters" and "the tree of life; which waters are a representation of the love of God; and I also beheld that the tree of life was a representation of the love of God" (1 Nephi 11:25). With this in mind, it is not difficult to understand why, in the book of Revelation, John described the throne of God as consisting of a river lined with trees of life: "And he shewed me a pure river of water of life, clear as crystal, proceeding out of the throne of God and of the Lamb. In the midst of the street of it, and on either side of the river, was there the tree of life, which bare twelve manner of fruits, and yielded her fruit every month: and the leaves of the tree were for the healing of the nations" (Revelation 22:1–2). What is more healing to the soul than the absolute conviction that one is loved?

Yet even those who have experienced the deepest types of human love cannot comprehend the love that exists in that better world. Isaiah wrote, "For since the beginning of the world men have not heard, nor perceived by the ear, neither hath the eye seen, O God, beside thee, what he hath prepared for him that waiteth for him" (Isaiah 64:4).

FINDING FULFILLMENT IN THE JOY OF OTHERS

I have over the years collected as much information as I can about my family. Some of my ancestors left wills, journals, testimonies, and life histories. I have found much in these to generate hope in my immediate family. In some of them are recorded experiences which the writers hoped would bless future generations. I have also tried to gather the testimonies and life histories of those who are still living to preserve their life-changing experiences that have power to edify and lift coming generations. Among these life stories is a dream that was written down by a father who believed his experience would give hope to his descendants. It has become an anchor to my soul through its description of the love of that better world:

"During one period of my life, I was saddened and discouraged. One night I dreamed I was standing at the gate of a beautiful city. There were no doors to this gate, and its wide opening seemed to invite all to enter. I could see through the gate the buildings of the city. They were all different, and yet the whole scene presented a wonderful picture of unity.

"I looked up the main street and saw a man and a woman walking toward me. They were dressed in white and were holding hands. There was an ageless quality about their faces, a look of eternal youth combined with great wisdom. Without any words being spoken to me, I knew they were my great-great-grandparents.

"They radiated peace and love. They were kind and gentle in their manner. They were united in their devotion to each other. There was happiness and contentment on their countenances. They passed through the gate and stood next to me. They told me it was a source of sorrow to them to see my sorrow. They knew me intimately—my life, my desires, my thoughts—and they had come to give me hope.

"They had discussed what they could do to make me happy. They had decided to show me something they believed would fill me with hope and joy. As this was communicated to me, I felt the wonderful warmth of their love and knew, without doubt, at that moment what celestial love entailed. It is a love that seeks the happiness of others and finds its fulfillment in the joy it imparts.

"They took me by the hand and led me through the gates of the city. We walked down the streets until we stopped in front of a building. Every line of this building reminded me of books and knowledge. My escorts told me, 'This is the library.'

"There was a front entrance, but, like the gate, it had no doors. We entered the main hall. It was open and spacious. There were no shelves in the center of the room, only along the walls. There were beautifully bound books on these shelves, which reached from the floor to the ceiling high overhead. There were more books than one could number.

"My hosts explained, 'These are the scriptures from all the worlds created by our Father in Heaven.' My heart filled with joy as I looked at them. What wonderful stories and truths they must contain. They allowed me to gaze on the volumes for a while and then said, 'We have discussed between us which verses in all these volumes we believe will give you the greatest hope.' They pulled a book from the shelf, opened it to a passage, and asked me to read. I read the most beautiful words I had ever looked upon. I began to weep and was filled with love and joy and hope that were overpowering.

"When I finished reading I awoke. I wish that I could write the words I read in the passage chosen by my ancestors, but I was not permitted to remember them. Yet, the hope they created within me has remained even to this day. I was permitted, however, to remember the subject of the verses. They spoke of the love of our Father in Heaven for all of his children, whoever and wherever they may be, his great desire that they be happy, and his preparations for their eternal joy. I believe that the purpose of every volume in that library was to testify of the love of God for his children, and I felt the assurance that joy would be granted. I do not know if such a room exists in reality, but the memory of it and the feeling I had while I read has been a constant source of hope and joy even in the darkest days of my life."

AN EARNEST OF FUTURE GLORY

Occasionally we get a foretaste of celestial love, and it may remain with us forever. Paul called these tastes of God's glory "the earnest of the Spirit" (2 Corinthians 1:22; 5:5). Earnest money is money that is given as an assurance that the rest will follow. It is usually only a small portion of the total sum. I am reminded of a truth taught by C. S. Lewis in one of his fantasy tales, *The Chronicles of Narnia*, which may illustrate Paul's words. After tasting the love of Christ, the children in the story described it in the following manner.

"Such a sweetness and power rolled about them and over them and entered into them that they felt they had never really

been happy or wise or good, or even alive and awake, before. And
the memory of that moment stayed with them always, so that as
long as they both lived, if ever they were sad or afraid or angry,
the thought of all that golden goodness, and the feeling that it
was still there, quite close, just round some corner or just behind
some door, would come back and make them sure, deep down
inside, that all was well" (*The Magician's Nephew* [New York:
Collier, 1970], 178-79).

"NOT WORTHY TO BE COMPARED"

In the New Testament, perhaps no one other than the Savior
understood the darkness and trials of this world as much as the
apostle Paul. In his letter to the Corinthians he said, "Of the Jews
five times received I forty stripes save one. Thrice was I beaten
with rods, once was I stoned, thrice I suffered shipwreck, a night
and a day I have been in the deep; in journeyings often, in perils
of waters, in perils of robbers, in perils by mine own countrymen,
in perils by the heathen, in perils in the city, in perils in the
wilderness, in perils in the sea, in perils among false brethren; In
weariness and painfulness, in watchings often, in hunger and
thirst, in fastings often, in cold and nakedness" (2 Corinthians
11:24-27).

Paul certainly knew the more painful side of human existence, but he also knew the glory of the Lord's eternal kingdom.
In the same epistle he said: "I knew a man in Christ above four-
teen years ago, (whether in the body, I cannot tell; or whether out
of the body, I cannot tell: God knoweth;) such an one caught up
to the third heaven. And I knew such a man, (whether in the
body, or out of the body, I cannot tell: God knoweth;) How that
he was caught up into paradise, and heard unspeakable words,
which it is not lawful for a man to utter" (2 Corinthians 12:2-4).

How would Paul compare the glory of the eternal worlds with

the sufferings of our present existence? He spoke of that very comparison while giving hope to the Roman Saints. "For ye have not received the spirit of bondage again to fear; but ye have received the Spirit of adoption, whereby we cry, Abba, Father. The Spirit itself beareth witness with our spirit, that we are the children of God: And if children, then heirs; heirs of God, and joint-heirs with Christ; . . . for I reckon that the sufferings of this present time are not worthy to be compared with the glory which shall be revealed in us. . . . For we are saved by hope: but hope that is seen is not hope: for what a man seeth, why doth he yet hope for? But if we hope for that we see not, then do we with patience wait for it" (Romans 8:15–18, 24–25).

Obviously Paul thought the joy, peace, and love of the "third heaven" was so far above the agonies he suffered in his life that they could not even be compared. The hope of that better world will enable us also to bear patiently whatever life will deliver.

"NOT EQUAL TO THE HUNDREDTH PART"

Not long ago we celebrated the sesquicentennial of the arrival of the pioneer company in the Salt Lake Valley. All over the world people reenacted the pioneers' exodus across the plains. We continue to be edified and touched by pioneer sacrifices and courage. Among all the pioneers, perhaps none suffered as intensely as those of the Willie and Martin Handcart Companies, who were caught in early snowstorms in Wyoming. Among the many experiences shared by Latter-day Saints who walked the plains of Wyoming many years later in honor of their ancestors, none touched me so deeply as that of a man whose wife's forebears had suffered in the Willie and Martin companies.

"We had just finished reading of the trials of the Saints at Martin's Cove," he said, "when we were invited to scatter throughout the cove to sit and ponder. I left the monument on the top of the hill and went down to a grassy spot among some trees and large rocks. I was deeply saddened by the tragedy that took place here over one hundred years ago. As I sat there, in my mind's eye I seemed to see a girl of about eleven or twelve standing before me dressed in pioneer attire. 'Don't mourn for us,' she said. 'Our suffering was not equal to the hundredth part of what we have received.'

"As her image faded in my mind, I thought of the promise the Lord made the Saints in Missouri, 'Ye cannot behold with your natural eyes, for the present time, the design of your God concerning those things which shall come hereafter, and the glory which shall follow after much tribulation. For after much tribulation come the blessings. Wherefore the day cometh that ye shall be crowned with much glory; the hour is not yet, but is nigh at hand' (D&C 58:3-4)."

Perhaps Joseph Smith said it best when he promised the Saints that "all your losses will be made up to you in the resurrection, provided you continue faithful. By the vision of the Almighty I have seen it" (*Teachings of the Prophet Joseph Smith*, sel. Joseph Fielding Smith [Salt Lake City: Deseret Book, 1976], 296).

"THAT SAME SOCIALITY"

An eternity drinking from the fountain of the Lord's love is rendered even more glorious with the knowledge that it can be shared with others we love and that our relationships do not end at death. Joseph Smith revealed: "When the Savior shall appear we shall see him as he is. We shall see that he is a man like ourselves. And that same sociality which exists among us here will exist among us there, only it will be coupled with eternal glory, which glory we do not now enjoy" (D&C 130:1-2).

My children have reached the age when they are going to college, leaving on missions, and setting up homes of their own.

How wonderful it is when they all return home from time to time to gather around the dinner table to laugh and share memories. Often, grandparents, aunts, uncles, and cousins share these moments with us. When I read the words of Joseph Smith in Doctrine and Covenants 130:1-2, I think of those times.

As Latter-day Saints we have the hope that these associations will endure and be amplified. What is true of our immediate families is also true of the broader family of God. Describing the latter-day Zion, "the Lord said unto Enoch: Then shalt thou and all thy city meet them there, and we will receive them into our bosom, and they shall see us; and we will fall upon their necks, and they shall fall upon our necks, and we will kiss each other; and there shall be mine abode, and it shall be Zion, which shall come forth out of all the creations which I have made" (Moses 7:63-64).

THROUGH THE MINISTRATION OF THE CELESTIAL

I recall teaching the beauty of these truths to a class of adults when a mother of a rebellious child remarked with great sadness that the thought of eternity without her child created a great depression. "Where is the hope for me?" she asked.

Several publications and numerous conference talks offer hope, as do several passages of scripture. First of all, there is always the chance of a change of heart. The Lord said, "If the wicked will turn from all his sins that he hath committed, and keep all my statutes, and do that which is lawful and right, he shall surely live, he shall not die. . . . Have I any pleasure at all that the wicked should die? saith the Lord God; and not that he should return from his ways, and live?" (Ezekiel 18:21, 23).

C. S. Lewis once remarked: "I believe that if a million chances were likely to do good, they would be given" (*The Problem of Pain* [Glasgow: Fountain Books, 1977], 112). Therefore, having faith in the Lord's wisdom and mercy, we will do what Elder Howard W. Hunter counseled: "Don't give up hope for a boy or a girl who has strayed. Many who have appeared to be completely lost have returned. We must be prayerful and, if possible, let our children know of our love and concern" (Conference Report, October 1983, 92–93).

One who is assigned to the terrestrial or telestial kingdom still has hope and the promise of joy and a measure of fulfillment.

Even the glory of the telestial kingdom is described as beyond our imagination. "And thus we saw, in the heavenly vision, the glory of the telestial, which surpasses all understanding" (D&C 76:89).

The revelations of the Lord tell us that those of a higher kingdom minister to those of a lower. Speaking of the souls of those who inherit the telestial kingdom, the Lord revealed, "These are they who receive not of his fulness in the eternal world, but of the Holy Spirit through the ministration of the terrestrial; and the terrestrial through the ministration of the celestial. And also the telestial receive it of the administration of angels who are appointed to minister for them, or who are appointed to be ministering spirits for them; for they shall be heirs of salvation" (D&C 76:86–88).

Joseph Smith transformed all of Doctrine and Covenants 76 into poetic form for William W. Phelps. The following stanzas correspond to verses 86 through 88:

> These are they that receive not a fulness of light,
> From Christ, in eternity's world, where they are,
> The terrestrial sends them the Comforter, though;
> And minist'ring angels, to happify there.
>
> And so the telestial is minister'd to,
> By ministers from the terrestrial one,

As terrestrial is, from the celestial throne;
And the great, greater, greatest, seem's stars, moon,
    and sun.

> (James R. Clark, *Messages of the
> First Presidency of The Church of Jesus
> Christ of Latter-day Saints*, 6 vols.
> [Salt Lake City: Bookcraft, 1965–75]
> 1:166).

What a wonderful word is *happify*. No matter which kingdom those we love inherit, beings from higher kingdoms will minister to them and see to their happiness. In light of the great sealing power of the temple, we can hope that those closest to them, and, therefore, perhaps most deeply concerned about their eternal happiness, might be permitted to help in the ministration. We will have to wait and see, but we can be assured that the desire to minister and "happify" in that manner must be pleasing to our Father in Heaven and his divine Son.

CHAPTER EIGHT

For behold,
I am a son of God,
in the similitude
of his Only Begotten.

−MOSES 1:13

HOPE IN OUR DESTINY

Perhaps the greatest truth of the Restoration and the one most conducive to creating hope in a human heart is our knowledge of the ultimate destiny of mankind. Here we speak not of that better world but of the people who will inhabit it. Brigham Young taught the early Saints, "Mankind are organized of element designed to endure to all eternity; it never had a beginning and never can have an end. . . .

"It is brought together, organized, and capacitated to receive knowledge and intelligence, to be enthroned in glory, to be made angels, Gods—beings who will hold control over the elements, and have power by their word to command the creation and redemption of worlds, or to extinguish suns by their breath, and disorganize worlds, hurling them back into their chaotic state. This is what you and I are created for" (*Journal of Discourses*, 26 vols. [London: Latter-day Saints' Book Depot, 1854–86], 3:356).

We do not ultimately belong to a human race; we belong to a race of the gods. This truth is so powerful that Satan has and will continue to do anything he can to destroy our belief in it. When the Lord emphasized to Moses by repeating three times that Moses was his son and was "in the similitude of mine Only Begotten" (Moses 1:6; see 4, 7), Satan tempted him with the following words: "Moses, son of man, worship me" (Moses 1:12). Moses, however, believed the Lord and was able to resist the temptations of the adversary because he had a solid understanding of who he was. "And it came to pass that Moses looked upon Satan and said: Who art thou? For behold, I am a son of God, in the similitude of his Only Begotten; and where is thy glory, that I should worship thee?" (Moses 1:13).

When we fully accept this soul-lifting truth, a hope is born within us which becomes a powerful motivation for righteousness and dignity. "Behold, what manner of love the Father hath bestowed upon us," John wrote, "that we should be called the sons of God. . . . Beloved, now are we the sons of God, and it doth not yet appear what we shall be: but we know that, when he shall appear, we shall be like him; for we shall see him as he is. And every man that hath this hope in him purifieth himself, even as he is pure" (1 John 3:1–3).

Small wonder Satan is so anxious to have us believe we are not the literal offspring of God, to belittle, negate, and destroy our self-awareness. When we understand who we are and what our eternal destiny is, we will strive to live up to our divine parentage. Not only will we endeavor to act as if we belong to the race of the gods ourselves but we also will treat others in the light of this knowledge.

THE DIVINE FIRE OF GOD IN THEIR EYES

I recall sitting in my first class at the University of Colorado in Boulder. I had heard the university was a liberal school, and I went to class rather defensive and judgmental. Toward the end of the class, I felt the Spirit offer me a challenge. "Look in the faces of each student in this class," it seemed to whisper, "and see if you can find a single person in whose eyes you cannot see the divine fire of their eternal Father still shining, however dimmed by this fallen world." I began looking into the eyes of each student. I could not find a single one whose face did not carry the promise of eternal worth.

As I left the classroom, I had learned a valuable lesson, but the Spirit whispered another challenge. "Now walk the campus," it urged, "and look into the face of every one you meet and see if you can find a person in whose eyes you cannot see the divine fire of their eternal Father still shining."

I walked the campus, looking into the faces of hundreds of young people. I could not find any in whose eyes the spark of eternal dignity had been extinguished. Since that day, I look into people's faces wherever I go. I have examined tens of thousands of faces, and I have yet to meet one who does not still carry the stamp of divinity, however dimmed by the world.

LOOK!

A teacher in the Church Educational System shared his testimony of this edifying truth and how it affected his teaching over the years. What is true of his understanding of the value and worth of his students is also true of each individual we meet.

"During my first year of teaching seminary, I taught two young men I could not control during my lessons. They seemed to delight in making my life miserable, and nothing I did proved successful. I often hoped when I had a really good lesson that the Lord would strike them with the flu so they wouldn't come, but it never worked. I didn't like those two young men and didn't have much hope for them.

"I had a dream one night about them. The three of us were in a prison compound. We were dressed in rags and layered in mud. I felt very uncomfortable and out of place. Suddenly, a small, dim, warm light began to radiate from an unknown source. I looked to see its origin, but I could not discover it, so faint was it.

"The light began to lift us out of the mud, slowly and carefully. I still could not discover its source, and after a while I became so engrossed with looking at the ground shrinking beneath me that I stopped searching for it.

"The light lifted us above the prison walls. On the other side of the wall was a beautiful green countryside. We were lifted higher and higher. The light became brighter, warmer, and more radiant. It seemed to flow through us and created a joy so intense I thought I could not bear it.

"As we rose higher, the details of the countryside disappeared until it became a blur of bluish green. In time I saw the edges of the continent appear. I watched the continent shrink until the edges of the earth came into view. The world slowly shrank to the size of a large ball backed by the dark blue of heaven. It grew smaller and smaller until it was just a pinpoint of light. At last it blinked out.

"All the time the wonderful light increased. As the earth disappeared from view, I looked up and saw in the distance a beautiful city. I saw a man approaching us from the gate of the city. He was dressed in white and radiated the light I had felt from the very beginning. He stopped when he arrived within a few feet of us. He studied us very intently for a moment or two and then, looking into our faces, he smiled.

"He said a single word, 'Look!' I looked at him—who else could you look at in such circumstances? He shook his head gently as if to correct my misunderstanding and then again smiled with great pleasure. He said again, 'Look!' I looked at him more intently and somewhat puzzled. He smiled again, shook his head, raised his hand, pointed at us, and said, 'Look!'

"I thought, 'Could it be possible that he wants me to look at myself?' I looked down. The rags and filth were gone. I was dressed in a white robe, just as he was. I looked at my two companions and their rags were gone. They, too, were dressed beautifully. More important, the light, the radiance, the warmth were coming from us just as it came from him.

"Ever since that day, I have approached my classes with a deeper sense of awe and reverence not only for the subject I teach but for those who have come to learn."

"THERE ARE NO ORDINARY PEOPLE"

One constant theme in the writings of C. S. Lewis is that of the destiny of man. Lewis felt all of Christianity directed one to the ultimate fulfillment of mankind: becoming like God. In a sermon delivered at the Church of St. Mary the Virgin in Oxford, Lewis eloquently expressed the hope of each child of God:

"The load, or weight, or burden of my neighbor's glory should be laid daily on my back, a load so heavy that only humility can carry it, and the backs of the proud will be broken. It is a serious thing to live in a society of possible gods and goddesses, to remember that the dullest and most uninteresting person you can talk to may one day be a creature which, if you saw it now, you would be strongly tempted to worship, or else a horror and a corruption such as you now meet, if at all, only in a nightmare. All day long we are, in some degree, helping each other to one or other of these destinations. It is in the light of these overwhelming possibilities, it is with the awe and the circumspection proper to them, that we should conduct all our dealings with one another, all friendships, all loves, all play, all politics. There are no ordinary people. You have never talked to a mere mortal. Nations, cultures, arts, civilizations—these are mortal, and their life is to ours as the life of a gnat. But it is immortals whom we joke with, work with, marry, snub, and exploit—immortal horrors or ever-lasting splendors. Next to the blessed Sacrament itself, your neighbor is the holiest object presented to your senses" (*The Weight of Glory and Other Addresses* [New York: Macmillan, 1980], 18-19).

We have touched on only a few truths relative to that better world we are encouraged to hope for, yet these truths are powerful in their ability to inspire us. With faith in an existence where love flows like a continuous river and where God's sons and daughters reflect the divine light of their Eternal Parent, we can face the opposition of a world where darkness prevails, searching constantly for every good thing and thus maintaining our hope.

CHAPTER NINE

Giving line upon line,
precept upon precept;
here a little, and there a little;
giving us consolation by holding forth
that which is to come,
confirming our hope!

−DOCTRINE AND COVENANTS 128:21

HOPE IN GOD'S EARTHLY KINGDOM

Although it is encouraging and comforting to hope for eternal rest in a kingdom of love and holiness, we also find hope in the Lord's earthly kingdom. This earthly kingdom is a reflection of the eternal one for which we are striving. President Gordon B. Hinckley has on numerous occasions directed our attention to the wonderful time in which we live. Recently he said: "And so, my beloved brothers and sisters, let us rejoice together now as we celebrate with appreciation the wondrous doctrines and practices which have come as a gift from the Lord in this most glorious time of his work. . . . Let us ever be grateful for these most precious gifts and privileges and act well our part as those who love the Lord" (Conference Report, April 1998, 4).

More than once I have wished I had lived during a past period, if only for a day, to witness some of the marvelous works of God. I would love to have been in the crowd at Bountiful the day the Savior descended to teach the Nephites or to have witnessed the mighty miracles that freed the Israelites from the power of Egypt. As if he anticipated such desires from future generations, Jeremiah put all such thoughts into perspective when he testified that the day would come when events even as wonderful as the Exodus would be eclipsed by the great latter-day work.

JEREMIAH'S TESTIMONY

"And I will gather the remnant of my flock out of all countries whither I have driven them, and will bring them again to their folds; and they shall be fruitful and increase. And I will set up shepherds over them which shall feed them: and they shall fear no more, nor be dismayed, neither shall they be lacking, saith the Lord. . . . Therefore, behold, the days come, saith the Lord, that they shall no more say, the Lord liveth, which brought up the children of Israel out of the land of Egypt; but, the Lord liveth, which brought up and which led the seed of the house of Israel out of the north country, and from all countries whither I had driven them" (Jeremiah 23:3-8).

What wonder the ancient Saints would experience if they could spend a day with us. So many things we take for granted would be a marvel for them. Ancient Israel had only one temple, but we will soon have more than one hundred. Anciently, only one man, the high priest, could pass through the veil of the temple into its most sacred precincts and only on one day of the year, but today all Saints are invited to pass through the veil of the temple into the celestial room as often as we desire.

Hundreds of missionaries serve around the globe, and the Church is established in many, many countries. We have in our homes books of scriptures our ancestors never dreamed existed, and we enjoy knowledge past prophets fasted and prayed many days to receive and to record for our benefit. Today, every worthy male may receive and exercise the priesthood, and every member of the Church is privileged to receive truth through the great gift of the Holy Ghost. Besides all this we have the promise that no apostasy will take these precious blessings away from us as has happened in other generations. The Church will never falter but will continue to expand its influence in ever-widening circles.

TESTIMONY IN A LOG SCHOOLHOUSE

During the dark days of the Missouri persecutions, Joseph Smith gathered priesthood bearers together in a one room log schoolhouse in Kirtland. Wilford Woodruff relates the lesson the Prophet Joseph taught the gathered men:

"On Sunday night the Prophet called on all who held the Priesthood to gather into the little log school house they had there. It was a small house, perhaps 14 feet square. But it held the whole of the priesthood of the Church of Jesus Christ of Latter-day Saints who were then in the town of Kirtland, and who had gathered together to go off in Zion's camp. That was the first time I ever saw . . . Brigham Young and Heber C. Kimball, and the two Pratts, and Orson Hyde and many others. There were no Apostles in the Church then except Joseph Smith and Oliver Cowdery. When we got together the Prophet called upon the Elders of Israel with him to bear testimony of this work. Those that I have named spoke, and a good many that I have not named, bore their testimonies. When they got through the Prophet said, 'Brethren I have been very much edified and instructed in your testimonies here tonight, but I want to say to you before the Lord, that you know no more concerning the destinies of this Church and kingdom than a babe upon its mother's lap. You don't comprehend it.' I was rather surprised. He said, 'It is only a little handfull of Priesthood you see here tonight, but this Church will fill North and South America—it will fill the world.' Among other things he said, it will fill the Rocky Mountains. There will be tens of thousands of Latter-day Saints who will be gathered in the Rocky Mountains. . . . This people will go into the Rocky Mountains; they will there build temples to the Most High" (Conference Report, April 1898, 57).

I once had the opportunity of visiting Kirtland and the site of the old log schoolhouse. There a colleague related that account of Wilford Woodruff. Because of his intense love of Church history, this good man enabled us to see with our imaginations that humble group of priesthood bearers, sitting on the wooden benches, listening to the Prophet. I could almost hear for myself the wonderful words of that prophecy regarding the future destiny of the Church.

That prophecy is being fulfilled today. We have ten million members in the Church, and there are stakes all over the world. New countries are opening up every year, missions are dividing, and we have more than sixty thousand missionaries preaching the gospel. The Lamanites are blossoming as the rose in Mexico and in Central and South America. The Book of Mormon has been translated into dozens of foreign languages, and the Latter-day Saints are a respected and favored people. We have beautiful temples all over America and in many foreign lands. Soon we will have more than a hundred temples in operation. The Church is indeed filling the earth.

And yet we "know no more concerning the destinies of this Church and kingdom than a babe upon its mother's lap. [We] don't comprehend it."

A great surge of hope welled up in my heart as I reflected on those words of the Prophet Joseph Smith. I have visited many scriptural sites in Israel and in America, but none have produced such a feeling of hope for the future as a wooded area in Kirtland where a fourteen-by-fourteen-foot schoolhouse used to stand.

IT "BECAME A GREAT MOUNTAIN"

Many ancient prophets besides Jeremiah learned about our day. Using various poetic images they all bore the same testimony. They saw that nothing would stop the progress of the Church. It would spread and flourish until it filled the whole earth, eventually delivering mankind from the power of the adversary.

Perhaps the best-known image is that of Daniel, who interpreted Nebuchadnezzar's dream, in which the Church was depicted as a stone "cut out of the mountain without hands." After knocking down the great image made of different metals which represented various kingdoms that would rise up and take power, the stone "became a great mountain, and filled the whole earth" (Daniel 2:45, 35). Daniel told the king that in the latter days "shall the God of Heaven set up a kingdom, which shall never be destroyed: and the kingdom shall not be left to other people, . . . and it shall stand for ever" (Daniel 2:44). When President Spencer W. Kimball encouraged us to lengthen our stride, I assumed it was to help the stone roll forward faster. Lately, however, I have wondered if the counsel was not also given because the kingdom is progressing so fast we are in danger of being left behind.

"OUR HOPE IS LOST"

Ezekiel was shown in vision a valley filled with dry bones: "Son of man, these bones are the whole house of Israel: behold, they say, Our bones are dried, and our hope is lost: we are cut off for our parts" (Ezekiel 37:11). Ezekiel was told to prophesy over the bones, commanding them to live. "Prophesy unto the wind, prophesy, son of man, and say to the wind, Thus saith the Lord God; Come from the four winds, O breath, and breathe upon these slain, that they may live. So I prophesied as he commanded me, and the breath came into them, and they lived, and stood up upon their feet, an exceeding great army" (Ezekiel 37:9-10).

Beyond the hope of the ancient Israelites, the great army of the house of Israel has risen up in the last days and continues to rise. It is an army filled with the Spirit and the breath of God. Nothing will hinder its destined march.

After the failure of Zion's Camp to return the Saints to Jackson County, Missouri, the Lord assured the Saints that his work had not been frustrated. They needed to be patient for the time being. "But first let my army become very great, and let it be sanctified before me, that it may become fair as the sun, and clear as the moon, and that her banners may be terrible unto all nations; that the kingdoms of this world may be constrained to acknowledge that the kingdom of Zion is in very deed the kingdom of our God and his Christ; therefore, let us become subject unto her laws" (D&C 105:31-32).

"THESE, WHERE HAD THEY BEEN"

Isaiah emphasized the image of the house of Israel as a "forsaken . . . and forgotten" woman (Isaiah 49:14). The woman is told by the Lord to "fear not; for thou . . . shalt not remember the reproach of thy widowhood any more. For thy Maker is thine husband; the Lord of hosts is his name; and thy Redeemer the Holy One of Israel; . . . for the Lord hath called thee as a woman forsaken and grieved in spirit" (Isaiah 54:4-6).

The main cause of the woman's grief is her barrenness. Yet, she is told by her husband to "enlarge the place of thy tent, and let them stretch forth the curtains of thine habitations: spare not, lengthen thy cords, and strengthen thy stakes" (Isaiah 54:2). All of this will be necessary because of the large number of children she will have.

Isaiah here compares the Church to a tent. As the gospel spreads, the cords are longer and the stakes are farther and farther away from the headquarters of the Church. Longer cords and more stakes are needed so that each member will find safety and shelter underneath the ever-expanding "curtains." Later Isaiah changes the imagery from that of a tent to that of a city or a beautiful temple. He speaks of "stones," "foundations," "windows," "gates," and "borders" (Isaiah 54:11–12). Wandering Israel, camping in tents, has been established in a great city. Within the walls of this city, "all thy children shall be taught of the Lord; and great shall be the peace of thy children" (Isaiah 54:13). Isaiah, when speaking of "Zion, the city of our solemnities" earlier, conveyed the hope-filled promise that "not one of the stakes thereof shall ever be removed, neither shall any of the cords thereof be broken" (Isaiah 33:20). This verse also suggests the permanent nature of the Lord's latter-day kingdom.

To instill hope and joy in the woman, the Lord tells her to "lift up thine eyes round about, and behold: all these gather themselves together, and come to thee. As I live, saith the Lord, thou shalt surely clothe thee with them all, as with an ornament, and bind them on thee, as a bride doeth" (Isaiah 49:18). The Lord directs her attention to the gathering children of Israel, who are as beautiful as a bride's wedding garments. So many gather that the children tell their mother, "The place is too strait for me: give place to me that I may dwell" (Isaiah 49:20). I have seen the splitting of wards and stakes in every state I have lived in. When a ward reaches perhaps eight hundred members, or a stake five to six thousand members, the people begin to say something very much like, "The place is too strait for us; give us place that we may dwell."

The woman sees her beautiful children begin to gather and spread out and responds with the following words: "Who hath begotten me these, seeing I have lost my children, and am desolate, a captive, and removing to and fro? and who hath brought up these? Behold, I was left alone; these, where had they been?" (Isaiah 49:21).

There have been times in my life when the power of Isaiah's imagery has truly struck home, and the hope his words engender has swelled in my heart. I was raised in southern California. Although the Church was not small there, I believe the largest body of young Latter-day Saints I ever saw gathered together in one place was about one hundred. When I was seventeen, I went to Brigham Young University. In those days, the university held an opening assembly in the old Smith Field House. We sat in groups according to our home states. The students from each state sang their state song and tried to out-sing all the others.

After each area had a turn, we were invited to rise as a unified body and sing "The Spirit of God" (*Hymns*, [Salt Lake City: The Church of Jesus Christ of Latter-day Saints, 1985], no. 2). I shall always remember that stirring moment. I was sitting at the very top of the bleachers, so I could see the entire student body. Here were gathered more than twelve thousand young Latter-day Saints. They believed in the same truths that I did. I thought, "We are invincible!" Tears came to my eyes, and my heart was full of gratitude to be one with such noble young people. Had I been aware of Isaiah's words at this time, I would have known that my heart was also saying, "Who hath begotten me these . . . who hath brought up these? Behold, I was left alone; these, where had they been?"

I experienced similar feelings at a Church Educational System symposium when all the missionaries at the Provo Missionary Training Center filled the floor of the Marriott Center, singing "Called to Serve," and also at the dedication of the Provo Temple, when I saw some of the twenty-five thousand handkerchiefs waving with the Hosanna Shout. No wonder the ancient prophets believed the work of our dispensation would eclipse even the mightiest works of the past.

"AS A DEW FROM THE LORD"

Micah also spoke of the unstoppable nature of the latter-day work. He compared the house of Israel to both a refreshing shower and a powerful lion. The softness of the first image is placed in contrast to the strength of the second to accentuate and highlight both aspects of the Church.

"And the remnant of Jacob shall be in the midst of many people as a dew from the Lord, as the showers upon the grass, that tarrieth not for man, nor waiteth for the sons of men" (Micah 5:7). Just as the dew cannot be stopped from forming or the rains from falling, no power on earth will stop the Lord's people from fulfilling their divine mission of spreading the truths of the gospel to all the earth.

Both dew and showers cleanse, enliven, and refresh the air and the plants of the earth. The gospel will also have this effect upon all those who are blessed by its ordinances and doctrines. Indeed, Peter called the Restoration itself "the times of refreshing" (Acts 3:19).

Micah's words are echoes of the Lord's words given to Moses many centuries earlier: "My doctrine shall drop as the rain, my speech shall distil as the dew, as the small rain upon the tender herb, and as the showers upon the grass" (Deuteronomy 32:2). In his great hymn of the Restoration, the Prophet Joseph Smith used the same imagery: "As the dews of Carmel, so shall the knowledge of God descend upon them!" (D&C 128:19). In a spiritually parched world, the restored truths of the gospel—like the gentle rains of spring—bring hope.

"AS A YOUNG LION AMONG THE FLOCKS OF SHEEP"

Micah's second image portrays as much vigor as his first image did gentleness and beauty. "And the remnant of Jacob shall be among the Gentiles in the midst of many people as a lion among the beasts of the forest, as a young lion among the flocks of sheep: who, if he go through, both treadeth down, and teareth in pieces, and none can deliver" (Micah 5:8). As the sheep have no power to stop the lion, neither will any force on earth have the power to permanently stop the progress of the Church.

This prophecy is placed in an even higher position in the literature of the Restoration: the Savior quoted it three times during his ministry to the Nephites (3 Nephi 16:15; 20:16; 21:12). His explanations of Micah's prophecy occupied a large part of his teaching on the second day. Before the last great battle that would end in the extinction of the Nephite nation, Mormon concluded his message to future generations with Micah's prophecy (Mormon 5:24).

Many Old Testament prophecies have multiple layers of meaning, and they all affirm that the Lord's Church will roll forward until, as Joseph Smith testified, "it has penetrated every continent, visited every clime, swept every country, and sounded in every ear, till the purposes of God shall be accomplished, and the Great Jehovah shall say the work is done" (*History of The Church of Jesus Christ of Latter-day Saints,* ed. B. H. Roberts, 2d ed. rev., 7 vols. [Salt Lake City: The Church of Jesus Christ of Latter-day Saints, 1932–51], 4:54).

When other institutions, organizations, governments, and gatherings fail, our hearts can remain at peace, secure in the hope created by the unfolding progress of the Lord's church throughout the world.

CHAPTER TEN

We might have a strong consolation,
who have fled for refuge
to lay hold upon the hope
set before us.

—HEBREWS 6:18

HOPE IN A CHANGING WORLD

When the sixth seal (which corresponds to our own dispensation) in the book of Revelation was opened, John described a world in upheaval: "There was a great earthquake; and the sun became black as sackcloth of hair, and the moon became as blood; and the stars of heaven fell unto the earth . . . and every mountain and island were moved out of their places" (Revelation 6:12–14). This prophecy was repeated, using slightly different words, in the Doctrine and Covenants: "Not many days hence and the earth shall tremble and reel to and fro as a drunken man; and the sun shall hide his face, and shall refuse to give light; and the moon shall be bathed in blood; and the stars shall become exceedingly angry, and shall cast themselves down" (D&C 88:87).

"ALL THINGS SHALL BE IN COMMOTION"

These prophecies are most often interpreted literally. I do not wish to suggest it should be otherwise, but usually prophecy has

97

both a symbolic, or figurative, meaning and a literal one. The earth will reel to and fro as a drunken man. What will the whole world be drunken with? Scriptural symbolism suggests it will be drunken "with iniquity" (2 Nephi 27:1), "with anger" (Ether 15:22), and "with blood" (Revelation 17:6). Just as a drunken man is out of control, so too will mankind in the last days stumble due to the effects of sin, anger, and hatred. We see evidences of this nightly in the news with reports of the murderous acts of one people trying to "ethnically cleanse" another people from off the face of the earth. Indeed, the moon itself will seem to be bathed in blood, so great shall be the death and bloodshed on the earth.

The great earthquake and the stars falling also suggest this will be a time when nothing is stable. Surely there is nothing as firm as the earth or the stars. In the ancient world men got their bearings from the stars. In the last days, however, morals, ethics, leaders, organizations, and nations will be unstable. In such a world, where can one find direction?

The apostle Paul further amplified the idea of all things being shaken when he wrote that God would "shake not the earth only, but also heaven. And this word, Yet once more, signifieth the removing of those things that are shaken, as of things that are made, that those things which cannot be shaken may remain" (Hebrews 12:26-27). Paul was quoting the prophet Haggai, who said, "For thus saith the Lord of hosts; Yet once, it is a little while, and I will shake the heavens, and the earth, and the sea, and the dry land; and I will shake all nations, and the desire of all nations shall come" (Haggai 2:6-7). The "desire of all nations" is the Savior, who has promised to come; but before he comes, everything that is not rooted on the solid foundation of truth will fall. The principal reason for this latter-day shaking, therefore, is to reveal to all the world those things that are eternal and therefore incapable of falling. When the shaking is over, what will remain standing?

In these days the sun will be "black as sackcloth" (Revelation 6:12). Black suggests mourning, as does sackcloth. Perhaps the sun itself, as it looks upon men, will mourn for the wickedness it sees, just as Enoch heard the earth mourn, "Wo, wo is me, the mother of men; I am pained, I am weary, because of the wickedness of my children" (Moses 7:48). Why would the sun hide its face and refuse to give light if it were not that the deeds of men are so terrible it does not wish to shed light on them? The "angry" stars "casting themselves down" also suggests to me a world so evil no orb of light wishes to shine.

In the ancient world, the tops of mountains and islands were most often used as places of safety. But John saw that the mountains and islands were also moved: "And every island fled away, and the mountains were not found" (Revelation 16:20). There would be no places of refuge or safety. Jesus described this time to his apostles as a time when there would be "upon the earth distress of nations, with perplexity; . . . men's hearts failing them for fear, and for looking after those things which are coming on the earth" (Luke 21:25-26). The Savior's words indicate men will feel there is no hope for the future. What is the cause of this lack of hope? Moroni, from the dust of his own destroyed civilization, gives to the modern world an answer: "There must be faith; and if there must be faith there must be hope; and if there must be also hope there must also be charity. . . . And if ye have no hope ye must needs be in despair; and despair cometh because of iniquity" (Moroni 10:20, 22).

The prophets and apostles saw our day as a time when "all things shall be in commotion; and surely, men's hearts shall fail them; for fear shall come upon all people" (D&C 88:91). In such a world there is a great need for faith, charity and hope—hope in that which is firm, stable, unchanging, and reliable. We often sing the very comforting plea in the hymn:

> Swift to its close ebbs out life's little day.
> Earth's joys grow dim; its glories pass away.
> Change and decay in all around I see;
> O thou who changest not, abide with me!
>
> (*Hymns* [Salt Lake City: The Church of Jesus
> Christ of Latter-day Saints, 1985], no. 166).

Only in the gospel do we find an unchanging firmness that holds steady during times when "all things shall be in commotion."

A SURE FOUNDATION

Occasionally we might feel some of the despair of which Moroni spoke. Recently I turned on the television to watch the news. Every channel spoke of the latest scandal in Washington. It appeared that neither party and few national leaders were concerned with principles; rather, daily public opinion polls seemed to dictate every move. There was bad news about the world financial crisis relating to the unsteady rising and falling of world stock markets. Peace efforts in many parts of the world were crumbling, and war was threatening other nations.

I changed the channel and saw the latest fashions in immodest clothing paraded. Another channel portrayed a husband and wife bitterly quarreling before the whole nation while the moderator spoke casually about adultery and divorce. I listened briefly to another man suggest that because truth and morality are relative, we should be tolerant and accept whatever moral standard another wishes to choose. Among all the channels nothing appeared stable or firm.

Early the next morning I attended the temple. I was struck

this time as I participated in the temple ordinances by how much peace and hope was generated in my heart as I listened to the same familiar promises and made the same covenants. The actions and words, the clothing and the ceremony, calmed my soul. Here was something that did not change from day to day or month to month. I witnessed a sealing and thought of the power of the words "for time and all eternity."

That evening I read the scriptures. Once again I felt hope generated in my heart with the familiar words and stories, the cadences and rhythms of holy writ. Here again was something that would not change. The next day was general conference. I listened to apostles and prophets teaching eternal principles. John, in Revelation, described the apostles as stars in the crown of the Church (Revelation 12:1). Here were stars that would not fall. We know we can get our direction from them and find the way.

CATCH HOLD OF THE ROD

I love the words Lehi used to describe what he saw in his dream of the tree of life. His words suggest a direction with something firm to hold onto: "I beheld others pressing forward, and they came forth and caught hold of the end of the rod of iron; and they did press forward through the mist of darkness, clinging to the rod of iron, even until they did come forth and partake of the fruit of the tree" (1 Nephi 8:24). In contrast to the firmness imparted to those who grasped the rod of iron, Lehi described others who "wandered off and were lost" (v. 23). He saw "multitudes feeling their way towards that great and spacious building" (v. 31).

How grateful we should be that we don't have to wander and feel our way through life. We know our direction. We can press forward. We can grasp the iron rod. Above all else we can build our lives "upon the rock of our Redeemer, who is Christ, the Son of God . . . that when the devil shall send forth his mighty winds, yea, his shafts in the whirlwind, . . . it shall have no power over you to drag you down . . . because of the rock upon which ye are built, which is a sure foundation, a foundation whereon if men build they cannot fall" (Helaman 5:12).

My favorite hymn of all is "O Say, What Is Truth," (*Hymns*, no. 272). I feel hope every time I sing it, especially the last two verses:

> The sceptre may fall from the despot's grasp
> When with winds of stern justice he copes.
> But the pillar of truth will endure to the last,
> And its firm-rooted bulwarks outstand the rude blast
> And the wreck of the fell tyrant's hopes.
>
> Then say, what is truth? 'Tis the last and the first,
> For the limits of time it steps o'er.
> Though the heavens depart and the earth's fountains
>   burst,
> Truth, the sum of existence, will weather the worst,
> Eternal, unchanged, evermore.

In a world where all things are to be shaken, our Father in Heaven has given us a legacy of truth. We need not despair because of the instability and change around us. We can hold to the hope that abides in eternal things.

CHAPTER ELEVEN

Are not two sparrows
sold for a farthing?
And one of them shall not fall on the ground
without your Father knoweth it.
Fear ye not, therefore;
ye are of more value than many sparrows.

–JOSEPH SMITH TRANSLATION MATTHEW 10:26-27

HOPE IN THE
GREAT MIRACLE OF GOD

My daughter spent six months in Russia. When she returned she brought back as souvenirs and gifts several sets of the little dolls that fit inside each other. One of the sets had fifteen different dolls, the smallest of which was about the size of a grain of rice. As I opened doll after doll to find yet a smaller one inside, I was reminded of one of the great themes of the scriptures, particularly of the Book of Mormon—a theme that provides hope. Let us look inside the various realms of God's kingdom and learn of one of his great miracles.

NUMBERED, KNOWN, NAMED

Each summer my family goes camping at Bryce Canyon. In no other place in Utah is the sky so clear. Nowhere else can so many stars be seen at night. All of these are the creations of the Lord. "Worlds without number have I created," the Lord revealed to Moses, "and I also created them for mine own purpose; and by the Son I created them, which is mine Only Begotten" (Moses 1:33). Though you and I cannot comprehend galaxies of worlds with our finite minds, the Lord is not so limited. "Innumerable are they unto man; but all things are numbered unto me, for they are mine and I know them" (Moses 1:35).

Isaiah assures us that not only does the Lord number and know the worlds but he also calls them all by name. "Lift up your eyes on high," Isaiah encourages us, "and behold who hath created these things, that bringeth out their host by number: he calleth them all by names, by the greatness of his might, for that he is strong in power; not one faileth" (Isaiah 40:26).

Notice the wonderful verbs that tell us of the Lord's relationship to the universe we see at night. His worlds are *numbered, known,* and *named,* because, as the Lord tells Moses, "They are mine."

I WILL VISIT YOU WITH THE "JOY OF MY COUNTENANCE"

Within the larger confines of space are single worlds. What is the Lord's relationship with each individual world? The Lord explained this to us in Doctrine and Covenants 88:

"The earth rolls upon her wings, and the sun giveth his light by day, and the moon giveth her light by night, and the stars also give their light, as they roll upon their wings in their glory, in the midst of the power of God. Unto what shall I liken these kingdoms, that ye may understand?" (vv. 45–46).

The Lord answered his own question with a parable:

"Behold, I will liken these kingdoms unto a man having a field, and he sent forth his servants into the field to dig in the field. And he said unto the first: Go ye and labor in the field, and in the first hour I will come unto you, and ye shall behold the joy of my countenance" (D&C 88:52). Each of the Lord's servants is given the same promise. Each in turn will receive the Lord's visit and be "made glad with the light of the countenance of his Lord" (D&C 88:56).

Not only did the Lord of the vineyard visit each servant once but he returned again and again. "Beginning at the first, and so on unto the last, and from the last unto the first, and from the first unto the last; every man in his own order, until his hour was finished, . . . that his lord might be glorified in him, and he in his lord, that they all might be glorified. Therefore, unto this parable I will liken all these kingdoms, and the inhabitants thereof—every kingdom in its hour, and in its time, and in its season, even according to the decree which God hath made" (D&C 88:59-61).

Even with the vastness of his creations, the Lord still visits each world and shares with its inhabitants the joy of his countenance. The Lord numbers, knows, and names all his worlds and visits each and every one, for they are his.

MANIFESTING HIMSELF UNTO ALL NATIONS

Within the larger confines of a single world are many nations. What does the Lord promise to do for each nation?

The title page of the Book of Mormon was written by Moroni. In it he reveals to us three major purposes of this sacred book. It will show "what great things the Lord hath done for [our] fathers." This implies that he will do the same "great things" for us. The second purpose is to help us "know the covenants of the Lord." The third purpose is the one we generally quote: "And also to the convincing of the Jew and Gentile that Jesus is the Christ, the Eternal God, manifesting himself unto all nations."

The Book of Mormon testifies that Jesus is the Christ and testifies of his willingness to manifest himself to all nations. The Book of Mormon is a record of one such manifestation. These manifestations vary according to the wisdom of the Lord. Every nation of the world today may find peace, secure in the knowledge that the Creator is desirous of manifesting himself unto them, showing them the great things he can do for them, and including them in his saving covenants. The Lord we worship numbers, knows, and names the nations of all his worlds, visits each, and manifests himself to every nation.

"MINDFUL OF EVERY PEOPLE"

Within a nation may be many different peoples, ethnic groups, and languages. What does the Lord promise to do for every people?

A most beautiful and inspiring story in the Book of Mormon is that of the four sons of Mosiah and their fourteen-year mission to the Lamanites. Reflecting on the mercy of the Lord, Ammon feels joy so great he "cannot say the smallest part which [he] feels" (Alma 26:16). He recounts the successes and challenges of their years among the Lamanites and then concludes with the lesson those years teach:

"Now my brethren, we see that God is mindful of every people, whatsoever land they may be in; yea, he numbereth his people, and his bowels of mercy are over the earth. Now this is my joy, and my great thanksgiving" (Alma 26:37).

When I served my mission in France, I, too, came to understand Ammon's testimony. There were many different ethnic groups in France. We taught the French, Italians, Algerians, Swiss, and others. I could feel the Lord's love for each of these people as we worked among them.

Since then I have had the delightful opportunity of speaking to the Polynesian people in the islands. On a recent flight, a young man next to me gazed out the window at the vast expanse of empty ocean and asked, "How do they find those tiny dots of land in all that water?" Even on a map it is sometimes difficult to locate the many tiny islands in the Pacific Ocean. His comment caused me to ponder the many times in the scriptures the Lord mentions the "isles of the sea." The Doctrine and Covenants begins with an exhortation that we "hearken" to God "whose eyes are upon all men," even those "that are upon the islands of the sea" (D&C 1:1). Isaiah spoke of the time when the Lord would recover his people from every nation and "from the islands of the sea" (Isaiah 11:11).

If the Lord is concerned about people on the tiniest spot of land, he is surely concerned about the many different peoples in a nation as great as Russia or China. If the Lord has blessed the peoples of Hawaii, Tonga, Samoa, Tahiti, New Zealand, and Fiji with temples, what hope does that blessing give the people of India or Indonesia? The God whose name we bear numbers, knows, names, visits, and manifests himself, and he is mindful of every people.

"HE REMEMBERETH EVERY CREATURE"

Within a people are many different individuals. What does the Lord promise to do for each individual soul?

Consider the story in the Book of Mormon of the conversion of Alma the Younger. After spending three days in the agonies of hell, Alma cried out to the Savior for mercy, which he immediately received. His pain was turned to joy, and his fear of God became longing for reunion. As he awoke from his three-day sleep, he expressed the thought that may be a central message of the Book of Mormon:

"I rejected my Redeemer, and denied that which had been spoken of by our fathers; but now that they may foresee that he will come, and that he remembereth every creature of his creating, he will make himself manifest unto all." Because the Savior remembers every individual soul, "every knee shall bow, and every tongue confess before him" (Mosiah 27:30–31).

The Savior who reminds us "the worth of souls is great in the sight of God" (D&C 18:10) numbers, knows, and names all his worlds. He visits each world, manifests himself to every nation, is mindful of every people, and remembereth every soul.

HE TOOK THEIR LITTLE CHILDREN ONE BY ONE

What does the Lord promise to do for each little child?

The first powerful lesson the Savior taught the Nephites when he visited them was the importance of each individual. When he descended from the heavens, the people fell at his feet. He commanded them to arise and "feel the prints of the nails in my hands and in my feet, that ye may know that I am the God of Israel, and the God of the whole earth." The multitude came forth to feel the tokens of the Savior's atoning sacrifice, "going forth one by one until they had all gone forth, and did see with their eyes and did feel with their hands, and did know of a surety" (3 Nephi 11:14–15).

If we had been in that multitude at Bountiful and were invited to approach the Savior to touch his hands, feet, and side, how might we have responded? Perhaps there were some in the multitude who knelt at his feet. Would he have hurried them on their way, reminding them that there were still hundreds left who needed to see him? I think not.

If we had been there, perhaps we would have embraced him and wept on his breast. Would he have firmly but gently pushed us away to make room for the scores who still were waiting? Perhaps there were some in the crowd who still felt the scars of past sins, who were struggling for peace and desirous of knowing if they had truly been forgiven. They would approach, anxious to hear some word or receive some touch that would assure them all was well. Would he not have seen that hunger and responded? He has all the time in the world for each of us. He is a one-by-one God.

After manifesting himself to the people, the Savior spent the day teaching them. As the day drew to a close, he said, "Behold, my time is at hand." He instructed them to return home and prepare for his return the next day. "And it came to pass that when Jesus had thus spoken, he cast his eyes round about again on the multitude, and beheld they were in tears, and did look steadfastly upon him as if they would ask him to tarry a little longer with them" (3 Nephi 17:1, 5).

Did Jesus tell them of all the other worlds, nations, and people he had to visit and teach? No. He said, "Behold, my bowels are filled with compassion towards you" (3 Nephi 17:6). They brought him their sick, whom he healed, and then he asked for their little children. Kneeling in the midst of the Nephite children, Jesus "prayed unto the Father, and the things which he prayed cannot be written" (3 Nephi 17:15).

He wept, telling the people that his joy was full. "And the multitude bare record of it, and he took their little children, one by one, and blessed them, and prayed unto the Father for them" (3 Nephi 17:20–21). Each little child is important to the Lord. Just as he blessed and prayed for each child, so do we bless and pray with our own children.

The importance of each child has come to me very forcefully at the birth of each of my five children. In those few sacred moments when I have been allowed to hold them for the first time, I have heard the quiet whisperings of the Spirit reveal to me truths about the characters and natures of my children. They are messages from their Father in Heaven about them, given as he transfers their care to that of an earthly father. For just a few precious moments two fathers communicate for the well-being of a newborn baby. What a difference it has made in our lives to know an Eternal Father is so personally concerned. This one-by-one focus is given a second witness when they receive their patriarchal blessings, and once again a Father communes individually with his children.

THE GREATEST MIRACLE

Many great miracles have been performed that demonstrate the wonderful power of the Father and the Son. The sick have been healed, lepers cleansed, sight restored to the blind, and the dead raised. The Resurrection itself is one of the wonders of God's great power. The Creation, too, is a miracle of beauty and order. Yet I cannot conceive of a greater miracle than to know that among the billions of worlds and the tens of billions of inhabitants on those worlds, each one is known and important to God and Christ. We need only to check the deepest places of our hearts to receive the confirming witness that this is true.

In descending order we have lined up the many tiny dolls my daughter brought home from Russia. They remind us that the God we love numbers, knows, and names all his worlds, visits each world, manifests himself to each nation, is mindful of every people, remembers every creature, and blesses each little child. Indeed, even the hairs of our heads are numbered by a God who knows when each sparrow falls. Whenever I touch the tiny doll at the end of the line, the doll who is the size of a grain of rice, hope is renewed in my heart.

CHAPTER TWELVE

Let thy mercy, O Lord,
be upon us,
according as we hope in thee.

−PSALM 33:22

HOPE FOR FORGIVENESS

Many stories in the Book of Mormon emphasize that the Lord is mindful of his children and remembers each one. The Lord does many things for his creations, for worlds, nations, peoples, or one tiny child. His greatest gift, however, centers on his atoning mercy, which he gives freely and immediately. In the scriptures, anyone who cries out for mercy is granted it. A few examples will serve as a testimony of this principle, with the assurance that what the Lord did for these people he will also do for us.

ENOS

When Enos hungered in his soul for a remission of his sins and the "joy of the saints," he knelt down before his Maker and "cried unto him in mighty prayer and supplication. . . . And there came a voice unto me, saying: Enos, thy sins are forgiven thee, and thou shalt be blessed. And I, Enos, knew that God could not lie; wherefore, my guilt was swept away. And I said: Lord, how is it done? And he said unto me: Because of thy faith in Christ" (Enos 1:3-8). Enos cried unto the Lord all day and into the night, and the Lord remembered Enos and manifested Himself unto him.

KING BENJAMIN'S PEOPLE

King Benjamin's people "all cried aloud with one voice, saying: O have mercy, and apply the atoning blood of Christ that we may receive forgiveness of our sins, and our hearts may be purified; for we believe in Jesus Christ, the Son of God." In response to their pleas, "the Spirit of the Lord came upon them, and they were filled with joy, having received a remission of their sins, and having peace of conscience" (Mosiah 4:2-3). The Lord knew these people, numbered them, and manifested himself unto them.

ZEEZROM

Although Zeezrom fought Alma and Amulek, when he realized his faults and expressed his faith in Christ, he, too, was remembered and blessed. Alma and Amulek found Zeezrom "upon his bed, sick, being very low with a burning fever; and his mind also was exceedingly sore because of his iniquities; and when he saw them he stretched forth his hand, and besought them that they would heal him. . . . And Alma said: If thou believest in the redemption of Christ thou canst be healed. And he said: Yea, I believe according to thy words. And then Alma cried unto the Lord, saying: O Lord our God, have mercy on this man, and heal him according to his faith which is in Christ. And when Alma had said these words, Zeezrom leaped upon his feet, and began to walk" (Alma 15:5-11). The Savior blessed Zeezrom, proving he was also mindful of his pains and desires.

KING LAMONI'S FAMILY

After hearing Ammon present to him the plan of redemption, King Lamoni "began to cry unto the Lord, saying: O Lord, have mercy; according to thy abundant mercy which thou hast had upon the people of Nephi, have upon me, and my people" (Alma 18:41). He was immediately answered. When he fell to the earth for three days, "the dark veil of unbelief was being cast away from his mind, and the light which did light up his mind, which was the light of the glory of God, which was a marvelous light of his goodness—yea, this light had infused such joy into his soul . . . that this had overcome his natural frame, and he was carried away in God" (Alma 19:6).

When he awoke and saw his wife, he, too, testified that the Savior was mindful and had manifested himself unto him. "Blessed be the name of God, and blessed art thou. For as sure as thou livest, behold, I have seen my Redeemer . . . and he shall redeem all mankind who believe on his name" (Alma 19:12-13).

The Savior was also mindful of Lamoni's wife. Her soul was lighted by the marvelous light of God's goodness. When she arose she "stood upon her feet, and cried with a loud voice, saying: O blessed Jesus, who has saved me from an awful hell! O blessed God, have mercy on this people" (Alma 19:29). The gospel message spread to Lamoni's father, whose beautiful prayer, "If thou art God, wilt thou make thyself known unto me, and I will give away all my sins to know thee" (Alma 22:18) was also immediately answered by the God who knew this king's heart, remembered him, and manifested Himself.

AMINADAB AND THE LAMANITES

Nephi and his brother Lehi were imprisoned by the Lamanites for preaching the word of God. When the Lamanites entered the prison to slay them, Nephi and Lehi were encircled with fire while the Lamanites were overshadowed by clouds of darkness. Full of fear, they asked Aminadab what to do. He replied, "You must repent, and cry unto the voice, even until ye shall have faith in Christ, who was taught unto you . . . and when ye shall do this, the cloud of darkness shall be removed." They did so, and the darkness was removed. "They were encircled about, yea every soul, by a pillar of fire. . . . And it came to pass that there came a voice unto them, yea, a pleasant voice, as if it were a whisper, saying: Peace, peace be unto you, because of your faith in my Well Beloved" (Helaman 5:41–43, 46–47). These Lamanites also were numbered, remembered, and blessed as the Savior manifested to them his great love.

These are but a few of the many examples of those who cried out for help and mercy. As Paul said, "Let us therefore come boldly unto the throne of grace, that we may obtain mercy, and find grace to help in time of need" (Hebrews 4:16).

ALMA THE YOUNGER

Of all the stories in the scriptures, none creates greater hope in my heart than the account of Alma. Alma had every opportunity to live a righteous life. He had the experiences of the previous generation to teach him the consequences of sin. His own father could tell him about life with King Noah, Amulon, and the wicked priests and thereby give him sufficient warning. His father had taught him of the mercy of Christ and raised his son in the righteous paths of the Church. Yet Alma rebelled. Not only did he rebel but he also sought to destroy the Church and led many people into the paths of his own wickedness. Could the Savior's mercy extend even to one who had no excuse for his unrighteous behavior?

After his confrontation with the angel, Alma described the state of his soul using very strong words: "I was racked with eternal torment, for my soul was harrowed up to the greatest degree and racked with all my sins. . . . I was tormented with the pains of hell; yea, I saw that I had rebelled against my God, and that I had not kept his holy commandments. . . . The very thought of coming into the presence of my God did rack my soul with inexpressible horror. Oh, thought I, that I could be banished and become extinct both soul and body" (Alma 36:12–15).

King Benjamin described the kind of torment Alma experienced as being like "a lake of fire and brimstone, whose flames are unquenchable" (Mosiah 3:27). Alma was drowning in that lake. Whenever I read the description of Alma the Younger's agony, I remember a time when I thought I was going to drown. My wife and I were caught in a very strong riptide off the California coast. I was struggling to help her to shore and became totally exhausted. When a wave rolled over my head, I thought I would never come up again. In desperation I reached up through the water, hoping I would feel something solid.

In a spiritual sense, I believe Alma did a similar thing. "And it came to pass that as I was thus racked with torment," Alma relates, "while I was harrowed up by the memory of my many sins, behold, I remembered also to have heard my father prophesy unto the people concerning the coming of one Jesus Christ. . . . Now, as my mind caught hold upon this thought, I cried within my heart: O Jesus, thou Son of God, have mercy on me, who am in the gall of bitterness, and am encircled about by the everlasting chains of death" (Alma 36:17–18).

I know of no scripture that gives the emotion and poignancy of hope quite like Alma's words. In agony and pain, drowning in guilt, desperate for something solid to cling to, he reached up and called upon a God he did not know, one he had only heard of. Maybe, just maybe, the God of his father might have mercy on one so undeserving as he, take hold of his hand, and pull him up.

I AM SNATCHED AND MY SOUL IS PAINED NO MORE

Isaiah tells us that "the Lord's hand is not shortened, that it cannot save; neither his ear heavy, that it cannot hear" (Isaiah 59:1). Anxiously, and filled with compassion, the Savior waited for Alma's cry. His ears were alert, and his hand was ready. When the cry came, the Lord did not hesitate. "The Lord in mercy," Alma said, "hath seen fit to snatch me out of an everlasting burning, and I am born of God. . . . I was in the darkest abyss; but now I behold the marvelous light of God" (Mosiah 27:28–29). What an appropriate word Alma uses. *Snatch* suggests a rapid response. Coupled with Alma's earlier expression that his "mind caught hold," a picture of hope can be formed. When I thought I would drown, how would I have felt when I reached up through the water if another hand had clasped mine in a tight grip and pulled me into the air? If I were an artist and wanted to paint a portrait of hope, I would paint that moment when Alma reached up, caught hold, and was snatched by the Savior's outstretched hand.

Only one other person in the scriptures describes the hope of the Savior's atoning love using the word *snatched*. Ammon, who shared Alma's experience, recalled his own memories of the day he discovered the hope of Christ: "Behold, who can glory too much in the Lord? Yea, who can say too much of his great power, and of his mercy, and of his long-suffering towards the children of men? Behold, I say unto you, I cannot say the smallest part which I feel.

"Who could have supposed that our God would have been so merciful as to have snatched us from our awful, sinful, and polluted state?

"Behold, we went forth even in wrath, with mighty threatenings to destroy his church.

"Oh then, why did he not consign us to an awful destruction, yea, why did he not let the sword of his justice fall upon us, and doom us to eternal despair?

"Oh, my soul, almost as it were, fleeth at the thought. Behold, he did not exercise his justice upon us, but in his great mercy hath brought us over that everlasting gulf of death and misery, even to the salvation of our souls" (Alma 26:16-20).

Ammon clearly believed he and his brothers deserved justice, but they were given mercy. The testimonies of both Alma and Ammon show the Lord "remembereth every creature of his creating, he will make himself manifest unto all" (Mosiah 27:30). If he will stretch out his hand for Alma and Ammon and his brothers, he will without doubt stretch it out to us. His ears wait for our cry, and his hand is ready to once again snatch a soul whose only hope rests in his mercy.

CHAPTER THIRTEEN

*For whatsoever things were written aforetime
were written for our learning,
that we through patience
and comfort of the scriptures
might have hope.*

−ROMANS 15:4

HOPE IN THE SCRIPTURES

The scriptures speak a great deal about hope, but even when not directly discussing hope, they create it. Indeed, one of their main functions is to inspire hope in all who read them. The title page of the Book of Mormon indicates that one of its major purposes "is to show unto the remnant of the House of Israel what great things the Lord hath done for their fathers." Why would the Lord be anxious for us to know what great things he has done for those of past generations? So that we may anticipate that he will do great things for us. In this manner every story in the standard works becomes a purveyor of hope.

If the Lord answered the prayers of others, he will answer ours. If he healed them, he will heal us. If he afforded them protection, he will grant it to us. If he sent prophets to them, he will send them to us. If he delivered them, he will deliver us. Because the Lord "is the same God yesterday, today, and forever" (D&C 20:12), we have great evidence for our hope in the stories of old.

"THEY MIGHT SET THEIR HOPE IN GOD"

The scriptures themselves tell us this is true. Before retelling the story of the Exodus, the writer of Psalm 78 explained why it was important to examine and reexamine this story: "I will open my mouth in a parable: I will utter dark sayings of old; which we have heard and known, and our fathers have told us. We will not hide them from their children, shewing to the generation to come the praises of the Lord, and his strength, and his wonderful works that he hath done. . . . That the generation to come might know them, even the children which should be born; who should arise and declare them to their children: that they might set their hope in God, and not forget the works of God, but keep his commandments" (vv. 2–7).

What is true of the story of the Exodus is true of every other account in the scriptures. The more familiar we are with them, the more hope they can generate. It is important to teach children as many stories as possible, so that the Spirit may bring to their minds in later years the right example from the past to produce the maximum brightness of hope.

A MEMORIAL FOR THE FUTURE

Sometimes the Lord specifically asked his people to create memorials of what he can do for his people. When the children of Israel ended their forty-year wanderings in the wilderness, the Lord stopped the flow of the River Jordan so they could pass into the promised land. The priests who carried the ark of the covenant "stood firm on dry ground in the midst of Jordan, and all the Israelites passed over on dry ground" (Joshua 3:17). The Lord then commanded Israel to "take you hence out of the midst of Jordan, out of the place where the priests' feet stood firm, twelve stones, and ye shall carry them over with you, and leave them in the lodging place, where ye shall lodge this night" (Joshua 4:3).

The pile of stones was to serve as a memorial to teach future generations of the Israelites' passage over the river: "When your children shall ask their fathers in time to come, saying, What mean these stones? Then ye shall let your children know, saying, Israel came over this Jordan on dry land. For the Lord your God dried up the waters of Jordan from before you, until ye were passed over, as the Lord your God did to the Red sea, which he dried up from before us, until we were gone over" (Joshua 4:21-23). The miracle the Lord performed for the older generation at the Red Sea he repeated with the younger generation at the River Jordan.

SPIRITUAL COUNTERPARTS

Many times as a teacher, a bishop, and a parent, I have seen the power a scripture story has to create hope in the hearts of those who are struggling. Often the Holy Spirit will direct our thoughts to the correct story. I recall a young man who had sinned deeply and felt there was little hope for him. He said, "My sins have made me unclean." His statement struck a chord in my mind, and together we turned to Matthew and read: "And, behold, there came a leper and worshipped him, saying, Lord, if thou wilt, thou canst make me clean. And Jesus put forth his hand, and touched him, saying, I will; be thou clean. And immediately his leprosy was cleansed" (Matthew 8:2-3). The Spirit bore witness to him that the Lord could do for him spiritually what He had done for this man physically. The young man left the office with a heart filled with hope inspired by a simple scripture story.

Sometimes we do not recognize the hope in each scripture story because we do not realize that physical miracles performed in the ancient world have spiritual counterparts in our own. Once I was teaching an Old Testament class. We had just completed the story of Elijah calling down fire from heaven to show the Israelites which god was the real God. A student asked, "Why doesn't the Lord perform these kinds of miracles today?" I was somewhat troubled over my failure to give him a satisfying answer and pondered his question.

As I reexamined the story, certain elements began to stand out. "How long halt ye between two opinions?" Elijah asked his people. It struck me that people today still struggle in choosing the right course to take. Every convert must make decisions similar to those faced by Elijah's people. Elijah proposed a test. Offerings were prepared and prayers were uttered. "The God that answereth by fire, let him be God," Elijah said. This great prophet then prayed for the people. "Lord God of Abraham, Isaac, and of Israel, let it be known this day that thou art God in Israel, and that I am thy servant" (1 Kings 18:24, 36).

God still answers by fire—the fire of the Holy Ghost. We encourage members and investigators to offer prayers to the Lord, promising them they will know by a burning in their bosom that he lives and who his prophets are. I realized that I had seen God answer by fire many times. I now had an answer for the young man in my class.

"I would like to see someone receive sight," another student once said. I was able to tell her that the Lord performs that miracle many times each day. We turned to the writings of Isaiah. When Isaiah prophesied of the coming forth of the Book of Mormon, Isaiah said that among other things that this great book would do "in that day shall the deaf hear the words of the book, and the eyes of the blind shall see out of obscurity, and out of darkness" (Isaiah 29:18). Is granting physical sight or physical hearing a greater miracle than restoring spiritual vision?

A couple in my ward once found great hope in the story of

Hannah. They, too, wanted children. Although their yearned-for blessing seemed long in coming, their hope never died. Finally, after the exercise of much faith and many prayers, the desired children came.

When hope is needed, there will be a story in the scriptures that will testify to our souls that the Lord will bless us as he blessed those before us. When we read the scriptures continually and frequently, the Holy Ghost can draw from their treasures the right application to create the greatest hope. Like the generations that followed Joshua, we must frequently return to the memorials created for us and remember.

CHAPTER FOURTEEN

Be not moved away
from the hope of the gospel,
which ye have heard,
and which was preached to every creature
which is under heaven.

—COLOSSIANS 1:23

THE CHALLENGE
OF THE ADVERSARY

In classic literature, over the gates of hell are written the words, "Abandon hope all ye who enter here." Part of the great agony of those who follow Satan is the destruction of all hope, leaving only fear and despair. One of Satan's titles is "destroyer." If Satan can destroy hope, he has essentially won the battle. He has already destroyed the hope of the third who followed him. It is his design to destroy hope among the living also. If we recognize that this is one of his chief ambitions, we can be forewarned and prepared to combat his enticings.

KORIHOR'S PHILOSOPHY

The scriptures suggest that one of the most powerful motivations for goodness and charity is the expectation or hope that through the atonement of Christ we can obtain a "better world" (Ether 12:4). Satan's objective, therefore, is to destroy both belief in Christ and belief in his eternal world of rest. Korihor was one of Satan's most effective agents in the Book of Mormon. His philosophy attempts to destroy all hope created by the truths of the gospel. The following statements constitute the foundation of many modern philosophies:

1. "Why do ye look for a Christ? For no man can know of anything which is to come" (Alma 30:13).

2. "Ye cannot know of things which ye do not see; therefore ye cannot know that there shall be a Christ" (Alma 30:15).

3. "Whatsoever a man did was no crime" (Alma 30:17).

4. "When a man was dead, that was the end thereof" (Alma 30:18).

5. "God—a being who never has been seen or known, who never was nor ever will be" (Alma 30:28).

The hope of the gospel is powerful against enticements such as these. Here we begin to understand why the scriptures suggest that hope offers us protection, much as a helmet does.

"ENGULFED BY FEELINGS OF HOPELESSNESS"

Elder Richard G. Scott spoke of a dream that illustrated to him in a very powerful way the desire of Satan to destroy all hope. It dramatically portrays the adversary's tactics and desires.

"Recently I awoke from a most disturbing dream. . . .

"In it I found myself in a very different and unknown environment. . . . I was anxiously seeking my wife, Jeanene. We had been separated, and I wanted very much to find her. Each individual I encountered said that I would not be able to do that. . . . I was emphatically told to forget her for she would not be found. . . .

"Then I was told, 'You are not the same. There is no individual by the name of Richard Scott, and soon all of the memories you've had of Jeanene, your children, and other loved ones will be eradicated.'

"Fear entered my heart, accompanied by a horrifying feeling.

Then came the thought: 'No, that is impossible. Those relationships are enduring and unchanging. As long as we live righteously, they cannot be eliminated. They are eternally fixed.'

"As more encounters came I realized that I was surrounded with evil individuals who were completely unhappy, with no purpose save that of frustrating the happiness of others so that they too would become miserable. These wicked ones were striving to manipulate those persons over whom they sought to exercise control. I somehow was conscious that those who believed their lies were being led through treachery and deceit from what they wanted most. They soon began to believe that their individuality, their experience, and their relationships as families and friends were being altered and lost. They became angry, aggressive, and engulfed by feelings of hopelessness. . . .

" . . . I broke out of that oppressive surrounding and could see that it was an ugly, artificial, contrived environment. So intense were the feelings generated by what I had been told by those bent on destroying my hope to take me captive that I had not realized the forces of opposition that made my efforts appear fruitless could have no power over me unless I yielded through fear or abandonment of my principles. . . .

"I can now understand that because of my faith in the truths of the gospel plan, I could break through Satan's manipulative, evil environment to see it as it is—not only in the dream, but in real life as well—a confining, controlling, destructive influence that can be overcome by faith in and obedience to truth. Others were disheartened, disoriented, and finally overcome as they lost hope because they either lacked a foundation of truth to engender conviction, courage, and confidence or they let their belief be overcome by the pressure of the moment" (*BYU Speeches, 1996-1997* [Provo: Brigham Young University Press, 1997], 357-58).

CALLING UPON GOD TO RECEIVE STRENGTH

When hope is destroyed, fear takes its place, and fear is an essential element of Satan's kingdom. He governs through it and captivates with it. When Moses confronted the adversary and rebuked him, "Satan cried with a loud voice, and ranted upon the earth . . . and it came to pass that Moses began to fear exceedingly; and as he began to fear, he saw the bitterness of hell" (Moses 1:19-20).During our times of despair we must remember the goodness of the God we worship and call upon him lest we be overcome by fear and despair.

When C. S. Lewis lost his wife of a few years to cancer, his faith was challenged, much as Elder Scott's was in his dream. Fear began to replace hope, and despair set in. During this dark period of his life he wrote: "I look up at the night sky. Is anything more certain than that in all those vast times and spaces, if I were allowed to search them, I should nowhere find her face, her voice, her touch? She died. She is dead. Is the word so difficult to learn? . . . But her voice is still vivid. The remembered voice—that can turn me at any moment to a whimpering child" (*A Grief Observed* [New York: Bantam Books, 1976], 16-17).

During those times when fear is greatest the danger of Satan's winning great victories in our lives is greatest. It was at a time of great fear in Moses' life that "calling upon God, he received strength" (Moses 1:20). Joseph Smith did the same thing in the Sacred Grove when he encountered the full force of the adversary. Joseph described how Satan tried to destroy all hope for deliverance:

"Thick darkness gathered around me, and it seemed to me for a time as if I were doomed to sudden destruction. But, exerting all my powers to call upon God to deliver me out of the power of this enemy which had seized upon me, and at the very moment when I was ready to sink into despair and abandon myself to destruction . . . just at this moment of great alarm, I saw a pillar of light" (Joseph Smith–History 1:15–16).

If Satan can get us to abandon all hope of deliverance or of mercy through the Atonement or of a better world where relationships continue throughout eternity, fear and despair become dominant, and we begin to taste the bitterness of hell. Bitterness of this type caused Alma to desire to "become extinct both soul and body" (Alma 36:15). However, like Moses and Joseph Smith, Alma cried out to the Lord and his fear was replaced with joy.

TRUSTING IN THE "ARM OF FLESH"

If Satan cannot destroy our hope through acceptance of philosophies like those of Korihor, he will seek to redirect our hopes to temporal things. "Why strive for the things of a better world," he suggests, "when you can have the riches and the pleasures of the present one?" If our hearts are set upon temporal things, when they fail us, despair can settle in and move us deeper into the devil's territory. Trusting in the arm of flesh is a deceptive policy. Nephi understood that truth and cried, "O Lord, I have trusted in thee, and I will trust in thee forever. I will not put my trust in the arm of flesh; for I know that cursed is he that putteth his trust in the arm of flesh" (2 Nephi 4:34). The arm of flesh inevitably fails, and one is left without a foundation and without hope.

That truth is beautifully illustrated in the Savior's parable of the prodigal son. After the younger son "had spent all . . . and began to be in want . . . no man gave unto him" (Luke 15:14, 16). When there is no more to take from you, the "arm of flesh" will abandon you. Only when he remembered his former home and father did the son's hope inspire his return.

Lest we be diverted by the pleasures, comforts, and riches of this world, we must keep a constant focus on the better world toward which we are striving. Moses found the strength to leave Egypt because he knew of a better reward than that which Egypt offered. "By faith Moses, when he was come to years, refused to be called the son of Pharaoh's daughter; choosing rather to suffer affliction with the people of God, than to enjoy the pleasures of sin for a season; esteeming the reproach of Christ great riches than the treasures in Egypt: for he had respect unto the recompense of the reward" (Hebrews 11:24-26).

The Lord has said, "There are many called, but few are chosen. And why are they not chosen? Because their hearts are set so much upon the things of this world, and aspire to the honors of men" (D&C 121:34-35). Nothing is quite as powerful in destroying the hope for an eternal world as satisfaction with the lesser things of this temporal world. That is why from time to time the Lord may try us by removing our temporal joys to help us seek comfort in more eternal ones.

"WE ARE ALL NAMED THE SAME"

Because I love mountains, I have always wanted to see the Swiss Alps up close. I once dreamed that I was standing on the balcony of a chalet deep in the Swiss Alps. I had traveled all the way from America just to see the sun set behind the mountains. I had only one day to fulfill my lifelong dream, so I was focused very intently on the peaks, hoping the clouds would clear.

Suddenly a noisy group of rather impish children with their toys came onto the balcony. They were very distracting, and in spite of my focus I could not help but look at them. Their antics were quite amusing. Soon my focus was broken, and I found myself staring at them and eventually sharing in some of their games. The clouds cleared, and the sun set beautifully behind the peaks, but I did not see it because I was too involved in the frantic activities of the children. After I had missed that which I had come so far to see, the children jumped up and ran off, but one turned long enough to say, "You never asked our names."

"What are your names?" I responded.

"We have only one," she said. "Terra. We are all named the same." With that she chased after the others.

I had served a mission in France, so the meaning of the name was as clear to me as the message. *Terre* in French means the earth or the world. We have come a long way to obtain celestial glory. If we win the battles of this life, we win everything. This is the last great test. Our desire must remain steadfast, but on this earth the splendor of the eternal worlds is veiled and only occasionally do we glimpse it. If we are not careful, the toys and activities of a fallen world may distract us, and our hope will be diverted when we lose sight of the truly beautiful.

CHAPTER FIFTEEN

Though I speak with the tongues
of men and of angels,
and have not charity,
I am become as sounding brass,
or a tinkling cymbal.

—1 CORINTHIANS 13:1

THE FRUIT OF HOPE

Faith, hope, and charity are so intricately interwoven that it is difficult to discern where one ends and the other begins. The scriptures, however, seem to teach that charity is the culmination of faith and hope. Paul taught, "Now abideth faith, hope, charity, these three; but the greatest of these is charity" (1 Corinthians 13:13). Whenever this holy trio is spoken of in the scriptures, charity always occupies the last position. But what exactly is charity? In its simplest definition, it is to love as Jesus loved. We know we are filled with charity when we speak, act, think, and feel as the Savior did. Jesus suffered long. He was kind. He did not envy. He was not puffed up. He sought not his own will but that of his Father. He was not easily provoked. He thought no evil. He did not rejoice in iniquity but rejoiced in the truth. He bore all things. He believed all things. He hoped for all things. He endured all things. Wherefore, my beloved brethren, if ye are not like Jesus, ye are nothing, for his love never fails.

Wherefore, cleave unto him. He is the greatest of all (see Moroni 7:45–46).

Why was the Savior able to do all these things? Mormon explains that it was due to his love: "Charity is the pure love of Christ, and it endureth forever" (Moroni 7:47). This love is two-fold. The Savior loves us, and he loves his father. His love for us is manifested in his willingness to sacrifice his life in our behalf. His love for his father is manifested in his perfect obedience to the Father's will.

To have charity is to live the Savior's quality of life, motivated by his degree of love. Our love for each other leads us to serve and sacrifice for each other. Because we love our Father in Heaven, we willingly obey all his commandments, for the Lord desires not just our obedience but our *loving* obedience. Joseph Smith taught that we need to know that our course of life is in accordance with the Lord's will. The pursuit of a Christlike life, a life of charity, gives us that assurance. Striving to lead a Christlike life adds substance to our hope.

FAITH, HOPE, CHARITY

Our hope also leads us to believe we can achieve a Christlike level of love. Mormon testified of this hope when he said, "When he shall appear we shall be like him, for we shall see him as he is; that we may have this hope; that we may be purified even as he is pure" (Moroni 7:48).

Our hope tells us there is a better world for which we were created, a world of indescribable glory and happiness. "In my Father's house are many mansions" the Savior taught. "I go to prepare a place for you . . . that where I am, there ye may be also" (John 14:2–3). Moroni testified, "I also remember that thou hast said that thou hast prepared a house for man, yea, even among the mansions of thy Father, in which man might have a more excellent hope" (Ether 12:32).

We have longed for this world all our lives, and it is possible to obtain it. Alma the Younger taught that we must live "having a hope that ye shall receive eternal life" (Alma 13:29). It is not sufficient only to believe it exists; we must have hope that it is possible for each of us to develop the perfect charity that is required to dwell with God.

Our faith in the Savior assures us that we can be cleansed of our weaknesses, follies, and sins through the Atonement. Even such righteous men as Nephi were troubled by what he termed "the temptations and the sins which do so easily beset me" (2 Nephi 4:18). We must have faith in the atoning sacrifice of Christ, and repent, trusting in the Savior's mercy as Nephi did. We will then receive a "remission of [our] sins, that [we] become holy, without spot," as Moroni testified (Moroni 10:34).

Knowing that the mistakes we make can be rectified through our faith in the Atonement, we "rejoice and exult in the hope and even know, according to the promises of the Lord, that [we may be] raised to dwell at the right hand of God, in a state of never-ending happiness" (Alma 28:12). We are prepared to develop charity. Mormon tells us to "pray unto the Father with all the energy of heart, that ye may be filled with this love, which he hath bestowed upon all who are true followers of his Son, Jesus Christ" (Moroni 7:48).

LOOK, LEARN, LISTEN, WALK

The development of charity will be a lifelong pursuit. Our faith in the Savior's atonement and our hope in achieving the final world of happiness must be constantly in our minds or we will become weary with the effort. In the Doctrine and Covenants we learn four simple words that will help us in our pursuit of a charitable character.

In an early revelation the Lord encouraged Joseph Smith and Oliver Cowdery with the following words: "Behold, I do not condemn you; go your ways and sin no more; perform with soberness the work which I have commanded you. *Look* unto me in every thought; doubt not, fear not" (D&C 6:35–36; emphasis added). Our first word is *look*.

Later, the Lord told Martin Harris, "*Learn* of me, and *listen* to my words; *walk* in the meekness of my Spirit, and you shall have peace in me" (D&C 19:23; emphasis added). Our second, third, and fourth words are *learn, listen,* and *walk.*

When we put our four words together, we have a formula for helping us to develop charity and become more Christlike.

The more we apply these four words to every situation of our lives, the more we act, speak, think, and feel like Jesus.

Undoubtedly we have all struggled to forgive another. We may desire to forgive but find it difficult to force forgiveness into our hearts. When these times come, the Savior ask us to listen as he pleads, "Father, forgive them; for they know not what they do" (Luke 23:34). He asks us to walk as he walked. When we ponder this great example of the Savior as we "view his death" (Jacob 1:8), the peace of forgiveness and the power of his love come into our hearts. Part of the majesty of the scriptures is in their ability to help us feel what we need to feel. We not only read the scriptures but experience them. That is especially true of those that speak of the Savior.

Sometimes we struggle with a specific commandment. We want to obey but it is often challenging. It would be much easier simply to walk away. At these times, the Savior's words come into our minds, asking us to look unto him and learn of him, listen to him, and pray, "O my Father, if it be possible, let this cup pass from me: nevertheless not as I will, but as thou wilt" (Matthew

26:39), and then to walk as meekly as he walked. There was a time in his life when he wanted to walk away, but even then he did not fail us. As we witness his agony in Gethsemane through the scriptures, knowing it was his love that enabled him to endure it, echoes of that same love reverberate in our own souls and we, too, can obey. We experience his obedience as we look, learn, and listen, and feel his own obedience born in our souls.

The world tells us in so many ways that we must look out for ourselves. When the voices of selfishness and ego whisper words like Korihor's when he claimed that "every man fared in this life according to the management of the creature; therefore every man prospered according to his genius, and that every man conquered according to his strength" (Alma 30:17), the Savior asks us to look unto him, learn of him, listen to his words: "He riseth from supper, and laid aside his garments; and took a towel, and girded himself. After that he poureth water into a bason, and began to wash the disciples' feet," telling them, "Ye call me Master and Lord: and ye say well; for so I am. If I then, your Lord and Master, have washed your feet; ye also ought to wash one another's feet" (John 13:4-5, 13-14). With these images fresh in our minds, we feel his humility born in us, and we can walk in the meekness of his Spirit.

Sometimes when I come home from work, I am tired and would prefer to be left alone for a while with a newspaper or the television. Often, however, one of my children wants to play a game or spend time with me. "Look, learn, listen to my words," I hear the Spirit whisper. I remember when the mothers brought their little children to Jesus. Though the apostles tried to keep them away, he said, "Suffer the little children to come unto me, and forbid them not" (Mark 10:13-14). I am then encouraged to walk as he walked. My irritation at being disturbed softens as I hear these words. I sense in my own heart his love for little children, and it is easy to turn my attention to the needs of my own children.

PUTTING ON THE IMAGE OF CHRIST

The scriptures are filled with hundreds more examples. There is something powerful in closely examining the life of Jesus and then trying to act as he did. Perhaps it is akin to children playing at being grown-ups or going to a costume party. When they dress up, they tend to act like the personality they are assuming. In time, for good or for bad, we become what we act as if we were.

Paul counseled us to "put on the new man, which is renewed in knowledge after the image of him that created him" (Colossians 3:10). As we identify with our Savior in this manner, we catch the Spirit of the Master, until Mormon's and Paul's definition of charity fits us also. It will take a great while to reach "the measure of the stature of the fulness of Christ" (Ephesians 4:13), but even the Savior himself "received not of the fulness at the first" (D&C 93:12).

CHAPTER SIXTEEN

The Spirit itself beareth witness
with our spirit,
that we are the children of God.

—ROMANS 8:16

THE SEEDS OF HOPE

William Wordsworth's poem entitled "The Rainbow" reflects on the power of youthful memories and the continuity they give to life:

> My heart leaps up when I behold
> A rainbow in the sky:
> So was it when my life began;
> So is it now I am a man;
> So be it when I shall grow old,
> Or let me die!
> The Child is father of the Man;
> And I could wish my days to be
> Bound each to each by natural piety.

The child is father of the man in the sense that the experiences of our younger years shape and mold our characters. We are most impressionable in the early years of our childhood. I believe the Lord is aware of how deeply memories of early events can be stamped upon our souls and uses those years according to his divine wisdom.

President Heber J. Grant taught this idea to all the teachers of children and youth. "There is no labor in which any of us can be engaged that is more acceptable in the sight of our Heavenly Father than laboring for the children in the Church of Jesus Christ. There is no question but that the impressions made upon the minds of little innocent children and young boys and girls have a more lasting effect upon their future lives than impressions made at any other time. It is like writing, figuratively speaking, upon a white piece of paper, with nothing on it to obscure or confuse what you may write" (*Gospel Standards,* comp. G. Homer Durham [Salt Lake City: Improvement Era: 1941], 73).

If we search our memories, we may find that our greatest hopes have roots in the experiences of our early childhood. Though later events may dispute the hope that was written in our hearts, the strength of those impressions will hold true in the face of great challenges. All the hopes that are most comforting to me were born in the first years of my life. Surely in each of our lives, a loving Father in Heaven has planted the seeds of hope.

"MORE LONGING FOR HOME"

The assurance of a better world and of a loving Savior came to me through the words of a sacrament hymn one Sunday evening when I was about seven or eight. I sat next to my mother, listening to her sing the hymn "More Holiness Give Me" (*Hymns* [Salt Lake City: The Church of Jesus Christ of Latter-day Saints, 1985], no. 131). The music caught my attention, and I joined in on the last verse. I began to feel things inside me I did not at that time understand. I felt such joy I wanted to continue singing long after the hymn was finished.

When we arrived home, I felt a need to be alone. I loved to climb trees as a boy. There was a large elm tree in our yard, and I climbed into its branches and softly sang the words of the last verse of the hymn over and over to myself.

More purity give me,
More strength to o'ercome,
More freedom from earth-stains,
More longing for home.
More fit for the kingdom,
More used would I be,
More blessed and holy—
More, Savior, like thee.

Two lines in this last verse pierced me to the very center: "more longing for home" and "more, Savior, like thee." As I sang these words, I felt an intense homesickness for a place where the Savior dwelt. I knew it was a place of indescribable wonder and happiness. I knew I had once lived there and that there were people there who loved me deeply. I knew I could go there some day if I would try to be like Jesus. I knew he would help me return to that home and that my whole life must be directed toward it. I wanted to be pure and holy like Jesus. So strong is the memory of this moment that I can still see the way the light softly filtered through the branches of the tree as the sun set. I can smell the elm leaves and feel the roughness of the bark in my hands as I clung to the limbs. I can hear the sounds of my mother and sisters as they went about their chores in the house below me, but they seemed so far away—as if we did not live in the same world.

I must have sung the hymn twenty or thirty times, until I was crying with the ache for my eternal home. When it finally grew dark, I climbed down and went inside. But I was a different boy. I had been baptized in hope. Whenever I sing that hymn now, hope for a better, more beautiful world, hope in the mercy of the Savior, hope in my own efforts to become like him, and hope in the love of an eternal Father in Heaven wells up inside me.

THE PILLARS OF HOPE

When I was young, we studied the Greek culture in school. We spent quite a bit of time on the different types of Greek architecture. I have long felt that the classic motifs and the pillars and triangles of Greek temples represent the highest architecture known to man. I used to dream of traveling to Athens to see the Parthenon. One year I found myself walking around this ancient wonder of the world, marveling at its beauty. I felt the massive columns that held the weight of the temple. For almost three thousand years they have withstood the forces of man and nature. Storms have not toppled them, nor earthquakes. I anticipate they will continue to stand for many more centuries.

The human soul is like a temple. In a sacred place deep within us our noblest and truest thoughts and feelings reside. Like the ancient Greek temples, the ceiling of that place is held up by massive pillars of strength and stability that can withstand the ravages, storms, and earthquakes of time. These are the pillars of hope. They were put in position by a gracious Father in Heaven and revealed in the pages of his holy books. They are strong to give all the other aspirations and righteous desires of our hearts a secure and a sacred place to dwell.

As I walk through the temple of my own soul, contemplating the strength of the pillars of hope shaped and positioned by the Lord, I feel deep gratitude, for hope is a brother to gratitude and both are silent witnesses of God's love, wisdom, and mercy. Whenever and wherever the human spirit is weighed down, it is comforting to know that within our souls is a temple of sanctuary and refuge. Strengthened by our visits to the Lord's own eternal temple, may these pillars of hope stand solid and true in our souls.

INDEX